Assisting the Beginning Teacher

Leslie Huling-Austin
Sandra J. Odell
Peggy Ishler
Richard S. Kay
Roy A. Edelfelt

Association of Teacher Educators
Reston, Virginia

Association of Teacher Educators
1900 Association Drive, Suite ATE
Reston, VA 22091

Cover design by Margaret S. Boebel, Chapel Hill, North Carolina
Text design, editing, and production by Edelfelt Johnson, Chapel Hill,
North Carolina

Library of Congress Cataloging in Publication Data pending

Contents

6 Starting a Beginning Teacher Assistance Program 95

Roy A. Edelfelt and Peggy Ishler

Appendix
Descriptions of Selected Beginning Teacher Assistance Programs 115

Foreword

The Association of Teacher Educators has long had a keen interest in the challenges faced by the beginning teacher. Although programs to address this phase of teacher development have been slow to arrive, public figures and educators now agree that the first years of teaching are critical. We are pleased to see this turn of events and feel satisfied that ATE's efforts to bring attention to the induction phase of teaching have begun to bear fruit.

The motivation for spotlighting the beginner is usually twofold: to induct the new teacher into professional practice and to assess the adequacy of the beginner. Both concerns are important. However, the latter one has tended to preoccupy legislators and citizens. We want to correct that imbalance. Many new teachers are not given a chance to show up well on an assessment because the assistance and the encouragement that a beginner needs and deserves are often not available.

ATE gave assessment the primary focus in the monograph *Teacher Assessment*, published in 1988, so we are not ignoring or devaluing efforts in that area. We see assisting beginners as one of the most productive ways to ensure that new members of the profession will succeed.

This volume is published by the association to communicate some of the best thinking on assisting the beginning teacher to those who will make decisions about and carry out the complex tasks of helping the novice. In June 1988 ATE's National Academy for Leadership in Teacher Education was privileged to bring together school- and college-based teacher educators and other members of the profession to showcase innovative models for planning and implementing induction and beginning teacher support programs. I asked some of the most thoughtful and knowledgeable people at that meeting to take us a step farther by putting their thoughts, knowledge, and experience on paper. This monograph is the result.

Billy G. Dixon
1988–89 President
Association of Teacher Educators

About the Authors

Leslie Huling-Austin is director of the LBJ Institute for the Improvement of Teaching and Learning and associate professor of secondary education in the School of Education, Southwest Texas State University, San Marcos. She was previously a program director at the Research and Development Center for Teacher Education at the University of Texas. There she was also principal investigator of the Model Teacher Induction project and coordinator of the Teacher Induction Network. Further, she managed the study, Teacher Induction in Diverse Settings, involving 26 institutions across the nation. Huling-Austin has written extensively in the field of teacher induction and has recently completed the chapter on teacher induction programs and internships for the *Handbook of Research on Teacher Education,* to be released by ATE and MacMillan in 1990.

Sandra J. Odell is director of the Elementary Graduate Intern and Teacher Induction Program and associate professor in the College of Education, University of New Mexico, Albuquerque. The program she directs was the 1985 recipient of the American Association of Colleges for Teacher Education's Distinguished Achievement Award. Odell's current research focuses on the needs and the concerns of new teachers in induction contexts, on the impact of induction programs on new teachers, and on retention.

Peggy Ishler is director of the Office of Field Experiences and Standards Compliance in the College of Education, Bowling Green State University, Bowling Green, Ohio. She chaired ATE's Commission on the Teacher Induction Process, which produced the monograph, *Teacher Induction: A New Beginning,* and is coauthor with Richard Kindsvatter and William Wilen of *Dynamics of Effective Teaching,* published by Longman in 1988. Her research is focused on teacher evaluation and the impact of induction programs.

Richard S. Kay is associate professor of educational psychology in the College of Education, Brigham Young University, Provo, Utah. He writes and lectures on self-concept development and socialization in professional settings. His writings have appeared in the *Journal of Psychology, Action in Teacher Education,* and the *Journal of Teacher Education.*

Roy A. Edelfelt is clinical professor at the University of North Carolina at Chapel Hill and a partner in Edelfelt Johnson, a consulting, writing, and editing enterprise based in Chapel Hill. A former teacher and professor at St. Cloud State College and Michigan State University, he also served for many years on the staff of the National Commission on Teacher Education and Professional Standards, first as associate executive secretary and then as executive secretary. From 1972 to 1981 he was senior staff associate in the National Education Association's Division of Instruction and Professional Development. He is the author of numerous articles and chapters and has edited many books. *Careers in Education,* his most recent publication, was published in 1988.

About This Book

The purpose of this book is to help practitioners and policy makers understand how important assisting beginning teachers is—and what it involves in terms of policy, procedures, pitfalls, personnel, price in time and money, and prospects.

Before the reader begins, an explanation of assumptions and definitions is in order.

Teaching and Learning to Teach

Teaching is a highly complex series of acts. It is not learned easily. Further, it cannot be done by formula or recipe. It is idiosyncratic. At the same time it must fit the learner, the context, and the knowledge or the skill being taught. Teaching behavior can seldom be transferred unchanged from one teacher to another. A technique or an approach that works for one teacher may not be effective for another.

There are, however, general principles of teaching. People who teach must be able to establish rapport with students. They must have skills in many aspects of teaching, such as organizing and presenting information, diagnosing students' abilities and needs, devising ways to assist students in concept development, leading discussions, asking questions, and evaluating students' learning.

Learning to teach cannot be accomplished entirely in college. It requires experience with students, at first in student teaching under close guidance, later in practice with advice and counsel from an experienced, highly competent teacher or supervisor.

The first-year teacher faces unique problems. The leap from college student to classroom practitioner is exceptionally wide. Teachers must not only be competent in their subject and know how to teach it; they must maintain a climate in which teaching and learning can take place. A teacher's personality is sufficiently exposed in teaching that his or her persona is almost transparent. This is a threatening, anxiety-producing situation for a novice, who is just beginning to establish a professional self-concept. Newly licensed teachers are prepared to *begin* to teach, but they are not thoroughly proficient. They are also not ready to fine-tune their competence without assistance and support. A complete conception and a realistic awareness of being a teacher cannot be gained entirely, simulated exactly, or understood sufficiently in preservice training. Even a superb student teaching experience lacks the completeness and the realism of a first teaching job.

The Need for Beginning Teacher Assistance Programs

A case must be made for beginning teacher assistance programs. The purpose, the process, and the other requirements of such programs are not well understood by lay policy makers or educators.

Beginning teacher assistance programs are part of a larger continuum of learning to teach. They must be considered in terms of what occurred before and what is apt to occur after the phase of teacher education they represent. Programs cannot realistically be specified in terms of time. Different beginning teachers take different lengths of time to achieve sufficient independence to function with only minimum support.

Programs to help first-year teachers will become much more in demand in the 1990s because of the huge number of teachers who will retire in the next few years. The time to develop and refine beginning teacher assistance programs is now, when the numbers are not so great as they are about to become.

Terminology

Certain terms are used consistently throughout this monograph, as follows:

Beginning teacher—a teacher who has not taught before; a novice, usually one who has just completed training to become a teacher.

Support teacher—mentor, pilot teacher, buddy teacher, helping teacher, coach, advisor, etc.

Evaluation—appraisal; a comprehensive process encompassing feedback and analysis of teaching (sometimes called formative evaluation) and assessment (often called summative evaluation), that determines tenure, employment, or certification.

Induction—a transitional period in teacher education, between preservice preparation and continuing professional development, during which assistance may be provided and/or assessment may be applied to beginning teachers.

Assisting and Assessing Beginning Teachers

Both assistance and assessment are essential activities to carry on with beginning teachers. Even though many state-mandated programs encompass both activities, the focus in this monograph is assistance because, of the two activities, it has been neglected.

The contention in this monograph is that assistance and assessment should be carried out by different (specially prepared) professional personnel. Assistance is clearly intended to provide nurture, help, and support to the beginning teacher and to foster analysis and evaluation of teaching for the purpose of improving teaching performance. Support teachers may serve assessment teams in summative evaluations as advocates of the beginning teacher.

Support teachers should be carefully selected and prepared for their role. Professional confidentiality is essential for an effective relationship between a support teacher and a beginning teacher. Maintaining the beginner's trust is necessary for open feedback and analysis of teaching between two professionals.

1

Beginning Teacher Assistance Programs: An Overview

Leslie Huling-Austin

The first year of teaching is tough. New teachers recognize that each year. Only recently has more time been spent and greater effort been given to helping the beginning teacher. Such attention has included orientation, assistance, and advice in the first year (or more) of teaching, a recognition that on-the-job nurture and support can accelerate success and effectiveness as well as prevent some beginners from giving up and dropping out.

Despite a solid college preparation, beginning teachers enter the real world of teaching and find that the challenges are more difficult than their collegiate study suggested. New teachers are suddenly on the spot to carry out full professional responsibility. Often they get the worst assignments and the heaviest loads. For many the first year is a sink-or-swim experience.

One remedy is to provide a gradual induction under guidance by one or more seasoned, highly qualified colleagues. The arrangement is unlike student teaching; both the beginner and the veteran are qualified professionals. But there is a difference between them. The beginner is inexperienced, often green, innocent, and naive. Many of the descriptors used in other professions are appropriate: *novice, rookie, neophyte, freshman, tenderfoot,* and *tyro.*

There is little doubt that assistance to the beginning teacher is part of a larger induction movement currently under way in this country. Although induction advocates say assisting the beginning teacher has been a long time in coming, compared with other educational trends, it has happened quite suddenly. Before 1980, most educators writing about teacher induction were from other countries, mainly Great Britain and Australia. Until quite recently, only a few isolated programs, most of them initiated by local districts or individual schools, were in operation in the United States. In 1981 Florida was the sole state with a mandated induction program. The movement has grown dramatically in this decade as a result of educational reforms that have swept the country. Today at least 31 states have either implemented or are piloting or planning some type of teacher induction program. The motivations for induction programs differ, though. Some proponents want primarily to assess beginners. Others want assistance and assessment, both clearly valid and compelling purposes. In a number of states induction includes the two processes. However, a conflict arises when the same personnel are used to assist and assess. Teachers are rarely open to consultation about problems and weaknesses with personnel who will also make employment or certification decisions.

In this monograph my coauthors and I go on record as (a) recognizing the importance of both assistance and assessment in the induction years, but (b) endorsing the separation of these two functions because they are inharmonious. The latter point will become more apparent as the reader proceeds.

Sufficient attention has been given to assessment of beginning teachers (ATE, 1987). The focus of this monograph, therefore, is assisting the beginning teacher.

In this chapter, I examine activity across the nation on assisting new teachers. First, however, I discuss the rationale behind assistance programs and their commonly accepted purposes and goals. Then I address the need to view assistance to the beginning teacher in the larger context of professional development and the need for program developers to design and implement programs that are consistent with the goals and the priorities of sponsoring agencies.

Reasons for Assisting Beginners

The way in which teachers move from preparation in college to teaching in schools hinders the kind of gradual induction characteristic of most other professions. In them, beginners gradually assume job responsibilities over many months (or even a few years) and have ready access to experienced colleagues for help as problems arise. Other professions use clerkships, internships, residencies, test status, apprenticeships, and similar experiences to induct beginners. The novice works under the guidance and the experienced eye of seasoned practitioners. In the best circumstances this involves observation and analysis, review and advising, testing and retrial, coaching and constructive assessment. The beginner has a chance to assume full professional responsibility gradually. The induction period bridges the gap between being a student in a professional school and being a functioning practitioner. It provides time to develop a self-concept as a professional, to be initiated into a professional culture, and to discover appropriate assignments.

In teaching, the novice assumes essentially the same job responsibilities that the 20-year veteran does, but on the first day of employment. Teachers are isolated from their peers for nearly all of the work day, further hindering induction. The lack of a gradual induction and the isolation that beginning teachers experience frequently cause them to learn by trial and error (Lortie, 1975). They develop coping strategies in order to survive. Unfortunately, evolved under stress and duress, such strategies may become the very ones that in the long run prevent effective instruction from occurring. An example my colleagues and I have reported (Huling-Austin, Barnes, & Smith, 1985) described a beginning teacher who had difficulty controlling students during class discussions, so she eliminated the discussions from her teaching repertoire. One can speculate that if the beginner is not given support and assistance, these early coping strategies can crystallize into a teaching style that may be used throughout the teacher's career (McDonald, 1980).

Another result of not providing support during the first year(s) is demonstrated by the high dropout rate among beginning teachers. The evidence is voluminous that without support and assistance many potentially good teachers become discouraged and abandon teaching (Ryan et al., 1980). Schlechty and Vance (1983) estimate that about 30 percent of beginning teachers leave the profession during their first two years. The overall rate of teacher turnover is 6 percent per year. The dropout rate of new teachers does not reduce to 6 percent until the fifth or sixth year. Forty to fifty percent leave during the first seven years. More than two-thirds of those do so in the first four years of teaching. In some states the loss of new teachers is even more alarming. In Indiana, for example, a statewide study found that 26.5 percent of beginning teachers dropped out within two years, 62 percent within five years (Summers, 1987). The poor retention rate of beginning teachers is especially depressing because there is evidence that the most academically talented leave in the greatest numbers (Schlechty & Vance, 1981).

The personal and professional well-being of beginning teachers is another reason that induction programs are needed. Any number of factors can cause difficulties for the novice, some outside his or her control—for example, an inappropriate assignment, excessively disruptive students, or culture shock in encountering students from different socioeconomic groups. Even in the most desirable circumstances, neophytes have problems. Of course, not all beginners experience personal and professional trauma, but many do. In any number of instances, beginning teachers lose self-confidence, they experience extreme stress and anxiety, and they question their own competence as teachers, even as people (Hawk, 1984; Hidalgo, 1986–87; Huling-Austin & Murphy, 1987; Ryan et al., 1980; and others). I contend (Huling-Austin, 1986b) that a profession has a responsibility for the well-being of its members as well as its clients and that not providing beginning teachers with personal and professional support when it is needed is professionally irresponsible.

The foregoing references document the need and the rationale for beginning teacher assistance programs. Across the country, legislators and educators are responding to that evidence by designing and implementing assistance programs. But a case still needs to be made with many educators and policy makers. Consequently goals and purposes for helping beginning teachers must be explicit.

Goals of Programs to Assist Beginners

Beginning teacher programs are as diverse as the agencies that initiate them, and purposes vary widely across programs. Some programs have a single purpose such as "to assist the beginning teacher in his or her first year of teaching," whereas others have a lengthy and sophisticated list of goals and subgoals. In my research (Huling-Austin, 1988), I have identified five goals that are typical, implicitly or explicitly, of most programs:

1. To improve teaching performance
2. To increase the retention of promising beginning teachers
3. To promote the personal and the professional well-being of beginning teachers
4. To satisfy mandated requirements related to induction
5. To transmit the culture of the school system (and the teaching profession) to beginning teachers.

Although these are certainly not the only goals in programs to assist beginning teachers, they can serve as a framework around which to design and establish program priorities.

National Attention to Beginners

Making a convincing case for the time and the money needed for a program to assist beginning teachers may require evidence beyond local data. Recent reports and studies can be instructive to any individual or group considering such a program. National commission reports, professional literature and activity, and state legislation have helped to advance policy and practice on beginning teacher programs in the country.

National Commission Reports

A number of national reports have addressed the issue. Among these are the *NCATE Redesign* (1985), the Holmes Group's *Tomorrow's Teachers* (1986), the Carnegie Forum's *A Nation*

Prepared: Teachers for the 21st Century (1986), the ATE's *Visions of Reform: Implications for the Education Profession* (Sikula, 1986), and the ATE's *Teacher Induction: A New Beginning* (Brooks, 1987). All five reports recommend a period of support for beginning teachers. This suggests that teacher induction is firmly planted in the national spotlight of educational reform.

Professional Literature and Activity

The literature in education also documents the increasing popularity of attention to the beginning teacher. For example, several major journals have devoted entire issues to the topic, including *Educational Leadership* (November 1985), the *Journal of Teacher Education* (January-February 1986), *Kappa Delta Pi Record* (July-August 1986), *Action in Teacher Education* (Winter 1987), and *Theory into Practice* (September 1988). The ERIC Clearinghouse for Teacher Education (1986a, 1986b, 1986c) has produced three digests on beginning teachers, *Components of Teacher Induction Programs, Current Developments in Teacher Induction Programs,* and *Teacher Mentoring.* Other noteworthy writings in the field include a selected annotated bibliography, *The Knowledge Base of Teacher Induction,* compiled by Johnston (1988), and a set of background papers entitled *The First Years of Teaching,* commissioned by the Illinois State Board of Education (Griffin & Millies, 1987).

The annual meetings of the ATE, the American Association of Colleges for Teacher Education, the American Educational Research Association, and the National Staff Development Council, to name a few, have devoted a number of sessions to the beginning teacher. The Research and Development Center for Teacher Education (R&DCTE) at the University of Texas at Austin focused several national conferences totally or partially on the beginning teacher (Griffin & Hukill,1983; Hord, O'Neal, & Smith, 1985; Huling-Austin, Putman, Edwards, & Galvez-Hjornevik, 1985).

A national Teacher Induction Network that includes people from local school districts, colleges and universities, state departments of education, regional educational service agencies, and national professional organizations was launched by the R&DCTE in 1983. The network currently is operated out of the Lyndon Baines Johnson Institute for the Improvement of Teaching and Learning at Southwest Texas State University.

The ATE's Commission on the Teacher Induction Process (1985 to 1988) produced a monograph on teacher induction (Brooks, 1987) and collaborated with the national Teacher Induction Network to produce a directory of teacher induction programs (Huling-Austin, 1986a). (Both publications are available from the ATE office in Reston, Virginia.) After the commission concluded its work in 1988, the ATE formed a Special Interest Group on Teacher Induction, which will continue to operate as a regular part of ATE. In addition, in 1988 ATE formed a new three-year commission to examine training for mentor teachers.

State Legislation

Despite three national surveys of state legislative activity conducted since 1985—by the ATE Commission on the Teacher Induction Process (Hawk & Robards, 1987), the Illinois State Board of Education (Eastern Illinois University, 1986), and the American Association of Colleges for Teacher Education (Neuweiler, 1987)—it is difficult to obtain up-to-date information on beginning teacher programs because the field is changing so rapidly.

The Illinois survey, which was the most definitive, found 17 states with programs for beginning teachers in the pilot or implementation stage; 14 states with programs in the study, planning, or development stage; and 20 with no programs or no current planning for programs. Of the states with operating programs, virtually all were established by mandate of the state legislature or the state education agency. Fourteen of the 17 included assessment for certification in their beginning teacher programs. In an additional state the program was to be linked to certification in 1988.

According to the Illinois report, program costs per beginning teacher varied widely, from about $100 in Georgia and North Carolina to $5,000 in the District of Columbia. Computing a valid average is questionable because data were unavailable for 5 of the 17 states and because the variables in some states' approximations were "soft." Among the programs reporting, the average expense per beginning teacher was approximately $1,300. In the data reported by the American Association of Colleges for Teacher Education in December 1987, only three states revealed no activity at the state level on teacher induction. This information clearly indicates that concern for the beginning teacher is sweeping the nation quickly, more so than most educational movements in recent history.

What Still Needs to Happen

Compared with a decade ago, there is great interest and considerable activity today in beginning teacher programs. The growing literature on the topic provides both direction and questions. State legislatures communicate the strongest and clearest message of concern for and commitment to beginning teacher programs. The group that appears to need the most convincing is the one closest to the problem—practicing educators in the public schools. Kilgore and Kozisek (1988) comment, "For the most part, school personnel are not aware of the literature or the effects they have on first-year teachers. Simply stated, principals and teachers treat novice teachers like they were treated, and have had no reason to think that things should be any different" (p. 11). In my opinion (Huling-Austin, 1988), "most of us assume that because more legislatures are mandating induction programs and programs are rapidly increasing in number across the nation, . . . there must be general consensus in the profession at-large about the need for and potential benefits of teacher induction. . . . [T]his is simply not the case . . . There is strong evidence that beginning teacher induction is not viewed as a pressing need in the field" (pp. 21–22). Of course, many teachers are leery of beginning teacher programs, seeing them primarily as arbitrary screening devices to weed out teachers who do not perform well according to state-imposed criteria, without adequate consideration of such factors as context, the reliability of observers, or the artificiality of performance in the presence of an outsider observing from the back of the classroom.

If programs to assist beginners are to succeed, school practitioners must recognize the needs of beginning teachers and the roles of experienced personnel in assisting them. In addition, those conducting programs must have the necessary resources to fulfill roles of assistance. Unless information and support are provided, programs have little chance of succeeding on a widespread basis. Perhaps Friske and Combs (1986) summarize the point best:

> Improving the quality of education can not merely be legislated. On paper, requirements can be met, yet still not effect true educational reform. . . . Without the commitment to the quality with which each [school practitioner] fulfills responsibilities to the beginning teacher and the teacher induction program, new teachers will merely be socialized into the existing system. (p. 72)

Moving Ahead: Fitting the Pieces Together

To have the desired impact, programs to assist beginning teachers need to gain the grass-roots support of the profession. It will also be necessary for such programs to be integrated effectively with both preservice teacher education and inservice staff development, so that teachers experience a continuum of training. In addition, beginning teacher programs must be designed to reflect the goals and the priorities of their sponsoring agency(ies). Part of making induction succeed requires fitting the pieces of teacher education together internally and externally.

Teacher Induction: Part of a Continuum

The beginning teacher phase of a teaching career is best understood in the larger context of teacher education, which is often described as a continuum.

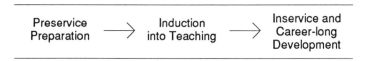

| Preservice Preparation | $\longrightarrow$ | Induction into Teaching | $\longrightarrow$ | Inservice and Career-long Development |

Viewed in this context, programs to address the beginning phase (i.e., beginning teacher assistance programs and internships) clearly need to function both as logical extensions of preservice programs and as points of entry into larger, career-long professional development programs.

It is important to have realistic expectations for beginning teacher assistance programs and to recognize that learning to teach is not a one-year (or two- or three-year) process. Expecting a beginning teacher program to produce polished professionals at the end of one year is unreasonable. Teachers spend their entire careers perfecting their teaching. Therefore, it is more important to provide a comprehensive, continuing professional development program at a rate and in a sequence that makes sense to each teacher.

Program Components

The breadth and the quality of beginning teacher assistance programs across the nation vary greatly. Some programs are comprehensive, whereas others are quite modest. Among the components that can be found in programs are the following:

1. Printed materials of employment conditions and school regulations
2. Orientation meetings and visits
3. Seminars on curriculum and effective teaching practices
4. Observation and analysis of teaching by supervisors, peers, and assessment teams, sometimes using videotapes of the beginning teacher's performance in the classroom
5. Follow-up conferences with observers
6. Consultations with experienced teachers
7. Support (helping/buddy/mentor) teachers
8. Opportunities to observe other teachers (in person or through subject-specific videotapes)
9. Released time and load reduction for beginning teachers and support teachers
10. Group meetings of beginners (for emotional support)
11. Assignment to a team teaching situation or a faculty team

12. Credit courses for beginners (university or district)
13. Beginning teacher newsletters and other publications designed to provide helpful tips for the novice teacher.

All of these features are not present in the large majority of programs, but they represent the building blocks, and most programs include some versions or variations of them. Rather than trying to build the "ultimate" program or to "plug in" a program that works well in another setting, developers need to select and use components that are likely to satisfy local priorities and can be implemented with the resources available.

References

Association of Teacher Educators, Commission on Teacher Assessment. (1987). *Teacher assessment.* Reston, VA: Association of Teacher Educators.

Brooks, D. M. (Ed.). (1987). *Teacher induction: A new beginning.* Reston, VA: Association of Teacher Educators. (ERIC Document Reproduction Service No. 279 607).

Carnegie Forum on Education and the Economy. (1986). *A nation prepared: Teachers for the 21st century* (Report of the Task Force on Teaching as a Profession). New York: Author.

Eastern Illinois University. (1986). *Final report for initial year of teaching study.* Chicago: Illinois State Board of Education.

ERIC Clearinghouse on Teacher Education. (1986a). *Components of teacher induction programs* (ERIC Digest). Washington, DC: Author.

ERIC Clearinghouse on Teacher Education. (1986b). *Current developments in teacher induction programs* (ERIC Digest). Washington, DC: Author.

ERIC Clearinghouse on Teacher Education. (1986c). *Teacher mentoring* (ERIC Digest). Washington, DC: Author.

Friske, J., & Combs, M. (1986). Teacher induction programs: An Oklahoma perspective. *Action in Teacher Education, 7,* 67–74.

Griffin, G. A., & Hukill, H. (1983). *First years of teaching: What are the pertinent issues?* (Report No. 9051). Austin, TX: University of Texas at Austin, Research and Development Center for Teacher Education.

Griffin, G. A., & Millies, S. (Eds). (1987). *The first years of teaching: Background papers and a proposal.* Chicago: Illinois State Board of Education.

Hawk, P. P. (1984). *Making a difference: Reflections and thoughts of first-year teachers.* Greenville, NC: East Carolina University.

Hawk, P., & Robards, S. (1987). Statewide teacher induction programs. In D. M. Brooks (Ed.), *Teacher induction: A new beginning* (pp. 33–44). Reston, VA: Association of Teacher Educators. (ERIC Document Reproduction Service No. 279 607).

Hidalgo, F. (1986–87). The evolving concerns of first-year junior high school teachers in difficult settings: Three case studies. *Action in Teacher Education, 8,* 75–79.

The Holmes Group, Inc. (1986). *Tomorrow's teachers: A report of the Holmes Group.* East Lansing, MI: Author.

Hord, S. M., O'Neal, S. F., & Smith, M. L. (Eds.). (1985). *Beyond the looking glass: Papers from a National Symposium on Teacher Education Policies, Practices and Research* (Report No. 7203). Austin, TX: University of Texas at Austin, Research and Development Center for Teacher Education.

Huling-Austin, L. (Ed.). (1986a). *Directory of teacher induction programs* (Report No. 7216). Austin, TX: University of Texas at Austin, Research and Development Center for Teacher Education, and the ATE Commission on the Teacher Induction Process.

Huling-Austin, L. (1986b). What can and cannot reasonably be expected from teacher induction programs. *Journal of Teacher Education, 37*(1), 2–5.

Huling-Austin, L. (1988). *A synthesis of research on teacher induction programs and practices.* Paper presented at the annual meeting of the American Educational Research Association, New Orleans.

Huling-Austin, L., Barnes, S., & Smith, J. (1985). *A research-based staff development program for beginning teachers.* Paper presented at the annual meeting of the American Educational Research Association, Chicago.

Huling-Austin, L., & Murphy, S. C. (1987). *Assessing the impact of teacher induction programs: Implications for program development*. Paper presented at the annual meeting of the American Educational Research Association, Washington, DC. (ERIC Document Reproduction Service No. ED 283 779).

Huling-Austin, L., Putman, S., Edwards, S., & Galvez-Hjornevik, C. (1985). *MTIP Satellite Conference proceedings* (Report No. 7209). Austin, TX: University of Texas at Austin, Research and Development Center for Teacher Education.

Johnston, J. M. (1988). *The knowledge base of teacher induction: A selected annotated bibliography*. Paper presented at the annual meeting of the Association of Teacher Educators, San Diego.

Kilgore, M., & Kozisek, J. A. (1988). *The effects of a planned induction program on first-year teachers: A research report*. Paper presented at the annual meeting of the Association of Teacher Educators, San Diego.

Lortie, D. C. (1975). *Schoolteacher: A sociological study*. Chicago: University of Chicago Press.

McDonald, F. (1980). *Study of induction programs for beginning teachers: Vol. 1. The problems of beginning teachers: A crisis in training*. Princeton, NJ: Educational Testing Service.

National Council for Accreditation of Teacher Education. (1985). *NCATE redesign*. Washington, DC: Author.

Neuweiler, H. B. (1987). *Teacher education policy in the states: Fifty-state survey of legislative and administrative actions*. Washington, DC: American Association of Colleges for Teacher Education.

Ryan, K., Newman, K., Mager, G., Applegate, J., Lasley, T., Flora, R., & Johnston, J. (1980). *Biting the apple: Accounts of first-year teachers*. New York: Longman.

Schlechty, P., & Vance, V. (1981). Do academically able teachers leave education? The North Carolina case. *Phi Delta Kappan, 63*, 106–112.

Schlechty, P., & Vance, V. (1983). Recruitment, selection and retention: The shape of the teaching force. *Elementary School Journal, 83*, 469–487.

Sikula, J. (Chair). (1986). *Visions of reform: Implications for the education profession* (Report of the ATE Blue Ribbon Task Force). Reston, VA: Association of Teacher Educators.

Summers, J. A. (1987). *Summative evaluation report: Project CREDIT*. Terre Haute, IN: Indiana State University, School of Education.

–2

Developing Support Programs for Beginning Teachers

Sandra J. Odell

Despite the recent focus on support programs for beginning teachers, much is not yet known about the development, the operation, and the assessment of such programs. Knowledge will eventually be gleaned from experience and research. Meanwhile, developers are eagerly seeking direction. What is known about programs that assist beginning teachers? The objective of this chapter is to answer that question and to provide guidance to those currently interested and involved in developing programs to assist beginning teachers.

An assistance-based program (Feiman-Nemser, Odell, & Lawrence, 1988; Fox & Singletary, 1986) to support and help beginning teachers in professional growth is based on several underlying assumptions:

- Beginning teachers, although well prepared in content and theory, still have much to learn about putting their knowledge to work.
- Providing new teachers with guidance, support, and assistance in analyzing teaching enhances their teaching effectiveness.
- Assisting the beginning teacher is good economy. It speeds up gaining full operational effectiveness for the new teacher and reduces the number who leave the profession out of disillusionment and frustration.

What follows reflects what seems to be working in contemporary programs designed to assist beginning teachers. Obviously those involved in developing a program need to tailor what is presented here to their own particular setting. No matter what that setting may be, however, goals for the program should be established. The needs of beginning teachers will have to be determined. Program support personnel will have to be selected, trained, and assigned responsibilities. And the program should be evaluated. Each of these aspects of developing a program for assisting beginning teachers is discussed.

Identifying Program Goals

The first step in designing a program to assist beginning teachers is establishing program goals. A variety of goals have emerged as support programs for beginners have been implemented across the nation. The core of all programs, though, is an emphasis on providing assistance to new teachers entering the profession. Educators know from personal accounts about the perils of first-year teaching. They know that many beginners have difficulty finding success in teaching, that new teachers facing the extensive responsibilities of becoming instructional leaders in classrooms have unique needs, that teaching requires a constant increase in teaching knowledge and skills, and that new teachers need help in becoming effective participants in the larger social structure of the school system. Accordingly, three primary goals of teacher induction programs seem appropriate:

1. To provide continuing assistance to reduce the problems known to be common to beginning teachers
2. To support development of the knowledge and the skills needed by beginners to be successful in their initial teaching positions
3. To integrate beginning teachers into the social system of the school, the school district, and the community.

Teacher educators view teacher development as a lifelong process that proceeds from preservice training for the student teacher, through an induction period of support for the beginning teacher, to inservice and renewal programs for veteran teachers. The assumption is that teachers will become continuously more sophisticated in knowledge, skills, and concerns related to teaching if they are given the opportunity to become lifelong students of the teaching-learning process (Burke & Heideman, 1985). More specific goals for an assistance program for beginning teachers are these:

4. To provide an opportunity for beginning teachers to analyze and reflect on their teaching with coaching from veteran support teachers
5. To initiate and build a foundation with new teachers for the continued study of teaching.

Statistics on teacher retention in the profession also influence goals for programs. Schlechty and Vance (1983) report that approximately 15 percent of new teachers are not teaching one year later. If current attrition rates continue, over 50 percent of today's new teachers will leave the profession in the next seven years. Part of the reason for the exodus is general disillusionment with teaching. More specifically, however, dropping out is causally related to the tremendous difficulty that beginners face in their first year. Often they are assigned the most difficult students, large classes, a heavy teaching load, extracurricular duties. Not infrequently, they must teach classes for which they are not prepared. The following two goals are suggested in recognition that beginning teacher assistance programs are not designed to address the larger, more general problems of the teaching profession. Instead, they are intended to make the first year of teaching more positive and satisfying and thus to boost retention rates.

6. To increase the positive attitudes of beginning teachers about teaching
7. To increase the retention of good beginning teachers in the profession.

Determining Beginning Teachers' Needs

A next step in developing a beginning teacher assistance program is determining the needs of the beginners in a particular context, so that appropriate and responsive support can be offered. In an extensive review of the literature on beginning teachers, Veenman (1984) identifies the perceived needs of beginners in schools where no assistance has been provided. He analyzed descriptive interview and questionnaire studies of teachers during their first year of teaching. In rank order, new teachers reported needing guidance and support in disciplining students, motivating students, dealing with the individual differences of students, assessing students' work, relating to parents, organizing classwork, and obtaining materials and supplies.

My work (Odell, 1986a, 1987) expands on the profession's understanding of the support needed by new teachers. Unlike Veenman's (1984) study, the research took place in schools where beginning teachers received assistance, and it involved direct observation of the needs of new teachers during their first year. Integrating these observations yielded a rank ordering of the needs of new teachers:

- Ideas about instruction
- Personal and emotional support
- Advice on resources and materials for teaching
- Information on school district policies and procedures
- Ideas for additional techniques on classroom management.

This rank order clearly implies that for new teachers to whom assistance has been provided, instructional needs are most important. In contrast, for new teachers to whom no assistance has been provided, needs related to managing students predominate. Attempting to understand this difference, I (Odell, 1986a, 1987) have hypothesized that by offering new teachers structured support at the start of their initial teaching year, school districts may help them diminish their discipline problems, with the result that new teachers, like veteran teachers, will be able to focus more on instructional than on disciplinary issues.

A number of hypotheses have been offered suggesting that practicing teachers progress through well-delineated stages of development (Burke & Schmidt, 1984; Fuller, 1969; Katz, 1972). In broad terms, teachers seem first to have concerns about surviving from one day to the next. From these they move to concerns about managing teaching responsibilities and then to concerns about the impact of their teaching on students. Eventually, experienced teachers raise questions about the teaching profession per se. By way of example, during the first stage of teacher development, teachers may ask, Will I be able to make it to the end of the week, or until the next vacation? How can I teach and do everything that is required and still have a life outside of teaching? More experienced teachers ask impact questions: Am I meeting the individual learning needs of my students? How is this teaching approach likely to affect students? Finally, veteran teachers ask broad questions: What are the advantages and the disadvantages of empowering teachers? What are the most current national issues related to teaching?

For the most part, beginning teachers move ahead steadily in their development as teachers. Progress seems to occur more rapidly when the system provides skilled assistance than when teachers are left to their own devices—a situation that beginning teachers have historically faced (Odell, 1987). In receiving support, new teachers seem to move beyond asking only questions related to survival, to asking questions about the impact of their teaching on their students (Odell, Loughlin, & Ferraro, 1987). Given that more sophisticated levels of teacher development are highly correlated with student learning, it is reasonable to conclude that programs to assist the beginning teacher serve to enhance student learning.

Selecting Program Personnel

A variety of personnel are needed to develop, implement, and evaluate a beginning teacher assistance program. Successful programs typically have a director or a coordinator who is responsible for the overall orchestration of the program. Sometimes support teams are formed (a district administrator, a university faculty member, and veteran teachers) to provide assistance. The school principal may be responsible for the evaluation of the program. The essence of any program, however, is the assignment of a veteran to serve as a support teacher for the beginner. Such support teachers have been identified variously as mentor teacher, clinical support teacher, buddy teacher, and advisor. In most programs (see the descriptions in the appendix) the support teacher continues full-time as a regular classroom teacher (sometimes with a lighter teaching load) while assisting one beginning teacher. In some model programs (e.g., a collaborative one between the Albuquerque Public Schools and the University of New Mexico, reported by Odell, 1986b; see also the appendix), support teachers devote their full attention to assisting several beginning teachers. No matter what the program structure, the support teacher is the key individual in implementing the program.

Establishing Criteria for Support Teachers

Given the critical role of support teachers, it is important to select them with care. Experience helps us identify the characteristics of veteran teachers that make them successful support teachers. These characteristics may serve as criteria for selecting support teachers.

Criterion 1. Demonstrated excellence in teaching. To have credibility with new teachers, support teachers must be excellent classroom teachers. Information about a potential support teacher's teaching effectiveness is available most directly from other veterans with whom they have worked as well as from principals and personnel officers.

Criterion 2. Demonstrated excellence in working with adults. Good teaching performance does not necessarily predict that a veteran teacher will function effectively as a support teacher. Veterans are sometimes inappropriately offered support positions solely on that basis. Support teachers must perform effectively as classroom teachers, but they must also work well with other adults, inasmuch as the target of support is the new teacher. There are also skills and knowledge required to guide the beginning teacher that are not necessarily attributes of the highly competent teacher of children or adolescents. Whether a potential support teacher meets this criterion can often be inferred from his or her success in working on school or community committees and from other experiences in working with adult learners.

Criterion 3. Demonstrated sensitivity to the viewpoint of others. One of the most difficult skills of the support teacher is the ability to appreciate another's viewpoint. The confident, competent teacher with extensive experience may, for example, have a tendency to be directive and prescriptive in working with new teachers. Many support teachers believe that new teachers will welcome suggestions once they have gained a modicum of teaching experience. However, successful support teachers become sensitized quickly to the fact that making dogmatic suggestions about teaching can be overpowering and intrusive to a new teacher. Indeed, the successful support teacher quickly establishes a climate in which strengths are recognized, viewpoints are respected, and the beginner's self-identified needs are central. The support teacher becomes a resource for working on those needs.

Even in a nurturing climate, new teachers often have difficulty in identifying their individual needs. A support teacher who uses effective questioning strategies can guide the beginner in identifying them without dictating explicitly the teaching behaviors that should be addressed. Helping the beginner in such self-evaluation is best accomplished when a support teacher recognizes and respects the viewpoint of the new teacher. A good support teacher is both a skilled questioner and a good listener.

The extent to which a support teacher is sensitive, has empathy, and is willing to entertain another's view can be assessed by talking with those who have worked with the veteran teacher. Written recommendations can be another source of data. Asking sources of data to address this criterion can be very helpful.

Criterion 4. Demonstrated willingness to be an active and open learner. Learning strategies for working with beginning teachers as well as strategies for acquiring knowledge about induction will add to the support teacher's effectiveness. Support teachers must be open to reading actively and attending training sessions to enhance their ability in the new role. Although past teaching experience provides support teachers with considerable appreciation for the art and the science of teaching, additional mentoring skills (e.g., reflective listening and coaching) and theoretical perspectives (e.g., stages of teacher development) should be learned. One means of assessing the achievement of this criterion is determining whether the support teacher has previously sought to study the teaching process and to expose himself or herself to the evolving knowledge base of teaching.

Criterion 5. Demonstrated competence in social and public relations skills. Support teachers interact with a variety of personalities, particularly if they work with more than one beginning teacher. Part of the support teacher's role is adapting to the new teachers and the administrators with whom they work. The support teacher's role is to interact in such a way that positive communications take place. This role is most effectively carried out by a practitioner who is personable, empathic, gregarious, caring, and adaptable.

Assigning Support Teachers to Beginners

Not all support teachers will be equally effective with all new teachers. Although it is not possible to predict with assurance how successful a particular veteran-beginner duo will be, there are some guidelines for assigning support teachers. Three are particularly important:

1. *Assign by grade level and content area.* A support teacher with experience at the same grade level and in the same content area as a beginning teacher has more credibility than does one with experience different from that of the beginner. Such a match may not be feasible in small school districts, where there is little overlap in grade level and content area among veteran and new teachers. In such situations it is particularly important that other means of enhancing the credibility of support teachers be found. For example, a special effort might be made to inform the new teacher about the support teacher's teaching excellence. Teaching has generic characteristics, that is, features common across all subjects. For instance, all teachers must stimulate students to think. Also, many problems that beginners face have little to do with content or level; examples are discipline problems and providing for individual differences.
2. *Assign by physical proximity.* In programs in which the support teacher is continuing his or her teaching responsibilities full-time while assisting a beginning teacher, every

effort should be made to house the new teacher next door or close by. If either the new or the support teacher must travel to the opposite end of the school grounds to meet, the likelihood of frequent or immediate support is diminished.

3. *Assign by teaching style and ideology.* Matching support teachers and beginners can be difficult. The goal is to create a productive, constructive relationship. Sometimes working with a veteran who shares a common view about teaching can result in such a relationship. The match may be in ideology, that is, a pair that favors a traditional teaching approach or a duo that prefers an innovative or informal approach.

A good match can be achieved by asking teachers to reveal their attitudes about teaching and the kind of relationship they believe might be most productive for them. In small school districts the best possible match should be made, even though the pool of support personnel may be limited. It is helpful to recognize that a likeness in philosophy and style is not necessarily the sole criterion upon which a relationship should be established. The best approach is to offer support teachers and beginners some choice in selecting the partner with whom they will work. If both beginner and veteran can choose, the chance of realizing a productive relationship is enhanced.

Determining the Responsibilities of Support Teachers

The primary responsibility of support teachers is to provide continuing, systematic support to beginning teachers. The process as well as the content of that support are discussed in detail in a later section of this chapter. This section is concerned with additional responsibilities that might be assigned to support teachers: providing orientation, conducting workshops and study groups, and writing newsletters.

Providing Orientation to New Teachers

Orientation sessions for new teachers typically occur early in the school year, often before students arrive. Although orientation to school district policies, procedures, and resources is an important part of joining the teaching force of a school district, beginning teachers are typically more interested in planning instruction for the start of school. Therefore, a minimal amount of time should be spent during orientation sessions for beginning teachers on matters unrelated to actual teaching. Policies, procedures, and available resources can be explained in take-home written materials or on an as-needed basis. Because the support teacher is available as a resource throughout the school year, school system information can be provided or reviewed as occasions arise, without the immediacy that seemed necessary before the beginning teacher assistance program existed. Classroom procedures, teaching activities, and the teaching environment are topics that provide useful content for the beginning teacher orientation sessions. A primary focus should be on planning for the first days of school.

Conducting Workshops and Study Groups for New Teachers

In addition to the continuing assistance provided to the individual beginner, some programs offer workshops that address planning and operational aspects of teaching relevant to all new teachers. Typically these workshops are led by support teachers and focus on topics that support teachers have identified in their work with beginners. However, workshops should also respond to the expressed desires and the expected needs of new teachers (e.g., parent conferencing, involvement of parents, referral procedures for special needs students, and security and legal issues).

Like veteran teachers, beginners find the opportunity to explore and share teaching ideas very useful. Therefore, it is essential to provide new teachers with the chance to participate in small group sessions. A desirable format is for support teachers to provide beginning teachers with content information such as is suggested above and then to ask them to work in small study groups in which an exchange of ideas is possible.

Writing Newsletters for New Teachers

In assistance programs involving many first-year teachers, a newsletter addressing topics of interest is sometimes provided by support teachers. An example is the monthly newsletter entitled *The Link*, published by support teachers in the Albuquerque, New Mexico, program. It serves as an additional means of connecting support and beginning teachers. The newsletter is a source of information (e.g., the time of the next workshop for new teachers), ideas, resources, and strategies for teaching.

Preparing Support Teachers

An essential step in developing and implementing a beginning teacher assistance program is preparing teachers to serve in a support capacity. Careful selection is a prerequisite to success, but the highest program priority is systematic preparation of support teachers. Thies-Sprinthall (1986) points out that "well-meaning but poorly trained" support teachers may pass on the "wrong set of the secrets of the trade" (p. 19). Sessions to prepare support teachers offer opportunities to increase knowledge about ways of assisting beginning teachers, to study the broad issue of induction into the school district (and into the profession), and to obtain ideas from others serving in a support capacity.

Determining Content of Training for Support Teachers

Given a careful procedure for selecting support teachers, program developers are likely to have enthusiastic and responsive learners in support teacher positions. The question then is, What training is necessary to increase the knowledge and the skills of support teachers? One essential area is the process of mentoring. Mentoring includes a number of components. The most important ones are enumerated below:

1. *Developing a trusting professional relationship.* As support teachers work with beginning teachers, it is crucial

that early on they get to know novices as individuals and develop trusting professional relationships. This is done most effectively outside of the teaching day and during a common planning time. During the initial phase of mentoring, it is necessary for the new teacher to understand that the role of the support teacher is not that of an evaluator, that the support teacher does not have any influence on employment-related matters. Rather the veteran-beginner relationship is one of studying the processes of teaching and learning together. Comprehending this point often relieves some of the anxiety that beginning teachers feel.

Support teachers frequently find it useful to meet new teachers somewhere off the school grounds to begin establishing a trusting professional relationship. The informal atmosphere of a coffee shop, for example, can create a level of comfort for the new teacher that makes getting acquainted easier than the more formal environment of the school does. The time it takes to build trust varies across teachers. Support teachers report, however, that a couple of informal sessions with new teachers typically allows each partner enough time to feel comfortable with the other. Spending informal time together early in the teaching year sets the stage for subsequent steps in mentoring.

2. *Determining the appropriate content of support.* After beginning and support teachers feel comfortable with each other (this may take some time), the support teacher can determine the areas in which the beginning teacher most needs assistance. My research (Odell, 1986a, 1987) has revealed that the categories of support in Table 1 are most often appropriate.

Support teachers should determine appropriate support for each beginning teacher on the basis of what the beginner identifies as a primary interest or concern. If a new teacher is unable to identify an area, the support teacher may ask questions that help the beginner reflect on performance. It might be necessary just to wait until the beginner is ready and able to recognize and articulate concerns.

Table 1
Categories of Support Appropriate for Beginning Teachers

Systems information	Giving information related to procedures, guidelines, and expectations of the school district
Mustering of resources	Collecting, disseminating, or locating materials or other resources
Instructional information	Giving information about teaching strategies or the instructional process
Emotional support	Offering support by listening empathically and sharing experiences
Advice on student management	Giving guidance and ideas related to discipline and managing students
Advice on scheduling and planning	Offering information about organizing and planning the school day
Help with the classroom environment	Helping arrange, organize, or analyze the physical setting of the classroom
Demonstration teaching	Teaching while the new teacher observes (preceded by a conference to identify the focus of the observation and followed by a conference to analyze the observed teaching episode)
Coaching	Critiquing and providing feedback on the beginning teacher's performance
Advice on working with parents	Giving help or ideas related to conferencing or working with parents

Note: Derived from "Induction Support of New Teachers: A Functional Approach" by S. J. Odell, *Journal of Teacher Education, 37*(1), 27.

A support teacher may notice, for example, that students in the beginning teacher's classroom are disruptive. Yet the new teacher may be unable to identify discipline as a problem or to admit that control is an area needing attention. The support teacher might then ask the beginner if students seem to move from one activity to the next without difficulty or whether all students pay attention when he or she gives directions for activities. Effective questioning helps the new teacher focus on trouble spots that the support teacher notices, and can lead the new teacher to recognize a problem area.

3. *Using coaching strategies.* Veteran teachers coaching other veteran teachers—that is, peer coaching—has been shown to be a useful strategy for improving teaching in other contexts (Joyce & Showers, 1982). Using the coaching technique with beginning teachers can also be an effective method of facilitating professional growth.

The steps in peer coaching can be adapted to a beginning teacher program. First there is a preconference, during which the beginner identifies a particular skill or strategy on which to focus during a teaching episode that the support teacher will observe. Following the preconference, the observation occurs, and the support teacher documents what happens by scripting, videotaping, or anecdotally recording it. A postconference ensues, in which the record is used to analyze the teaching episode. The postconference provides a time for the new teacher to describe his or her perceptions and feelings about the teaching episode. These cover such information as what students were doing during the teaching episode, whether intended purposes were being accomplished, what the teacher would do similarly or differently in the future, and what the teacher learned from the process. The degree to which all this can happen in such a complex interaction depends on the skills, the abilities, and the attitudes of both teachers and the relationship between them.

The emphasis in coaching as a support strategy is on what the beginning teacher thinks and feels, not on what the support teacher thinks. The new teacher should have the freedom to reflect fully on the teaching episode. This can occur if the new teacher, not the support teacher, directs the analysis, or if the support teacher asks questions and offers feedback. How this evolves depends on the veteran-beginner relationship.

Finally, the analysis of teaching should remain nonjudgmental on the part of the support teacher in the sense that it should not entail a summative assessment. An important product of the coaching approach with new teachers is the cumulative data on teaching that result. The data can serve as benchmarks against which to recognize progress and as empirical bases for the future development of the new teacher.

4. *Facilitating independence.* There is no clearly optimal duration for assistance to the beginning teacher. Most programs of structured support occur for only the first year of teaching; a few others last for two or three years (e.g., one in Virginia and one in West Virginia, respectively; see the appendix). Although programs of longer duration would seem to be more desirable, there are clearly diminishing returns over time, and cost often mitigates against extended periods of support. Accordingly, most programs aim at facilitating the independence (or self-sufficiency) of beginning teachers in one or two years. Few teachers, however, are ever completely independent. It may be more accurate to say that teachers become largely self-sufficient, because in healthy school faculties there remains great interdependence among teachers. Several authors (e.g., Bacharach, Bauer, & Shedd, 1986; Watts, 1986) have reported that teachers value consultation with other teachers as one of the top three sources of job-related knowledge and skills. This suggests a kind of never-ending interdependence.

Support teachers can help beginning teachers create their own support networks by encouraging them to build relationships with other teachers. Support teachers can also facilitate new teachers' self-sufficiency by familiarizing them with the many resources of the district and by encouraging them to seek personal support outside their jobs.

An addendum to the foregoing is that support teachers will best assimilate training regarding mentoring if they are versed in the empirical literature on the beginning teacher and the theoretical literature on stages of teacher development (and the whole process of induction into the profession). The best mentor, all else being equal, will necessarily be the one who most fully understands the needs and the nature of the new teacher.

Two other areas of training for support teachers are important adjuncts to becoming knowledgeable on supervision—effective teaching and effective communication. Training in effective teaching is useful to support teachers inasmuch as it can provide a framework to help guide them as they discuss the process of teaching with beginners. One qualification here is that support teachers should avoid the trap of simplifying or minimizing the complexity of classroom teaching by inappropriately reducing effective teaching to a checklist of appropriate behaviors, especially because this lends itself too readily to an assessment of beginning teachers by support teachers.

With respect to effective communication, support teachers are often in a position that requires the ability to communicate effectively with a variety of people—beginning teachers, other support teachers, higher education personnel, parents, and school administrators. Learning appropriate, effective communication skills and techniques of conflict resolution allows support teachers to work more productively.

Identifying Resources for Training Support Teachers

Many programs (e.g., in Arizona, Indiana, New Mexico, North Carolina, and Virginia; see the appendix) have involved university faculty in the training of support teachers. The Albuquerque program involves a faculty member from the University of New Mexico as director of the teacher induction program. Her duties include offering training courses to support teachers. Other programs use school district and intermediate school district resource personnel to conduct training sessions for support teachers. At North Carolina State University a faculty member has a joint appointment with the university and the Wake County School District to coordinate the beginning teacher assistance program. Recently ATE formed a National Commission on the Role and Preparation of Mentor Teachers. The commission will soon offer additional information that should prove helpful to those responsible for training support teachers.

Recognizing Benefits for Support Teachers

There are inherent benefits in the role of support teacher that motivate veteran teachers to become involved, whether or not programs require support teachers to continue their responsibilities as classroom teachers. Support teachers express satisfaction that the role offers opportunities to share information about teaching practice. Discussing teaching issues with beginning teachers seems to help support teachers better define the rationale for their own teaching. Training sessions for support teachers provide new information about the teaching-learning process and about working effectively as mentors. Support teachers frequently report that the training they receive for their role makes them more aware of the developmental process of becoming an effective teacher. Working closely with new teachers also gives them experience in practicing communication skills. They find that these skills generalize to other interactions in their professional lives.

Support teachers who are released (for a year or two) from classroom teaching to work with beginning teachers in several schools often experience additional benefits. They report that activities such as keeping track of materials, conducting pre- and postconferences, organizing workshops, moving from one school building to another, and advising on materials increase their organizational skills.

Support teachers working with several new teachers find an opportunity to broaden their view of effective teaching and to increase their appreciation of a diversity of teaching styles. An elementary school support teacher, for example, reported, "Although I believe in a much more formal teaching setting for my own work with children, some of the new teachers have informal settings and styles that seem very effective for young children."

Support teachers working in a variety of schools report that they also become increasingly aware of the diversity across settings. They discover that different socioeconomic levels, different leadership styles, and different facilities are factors that contribute to creating diverse school contexts. This expanded perspective helps them better understand decisions that the central office administrators make.

Establishing Incentives for Support Teachers

In addition to intrinsic satisfactions, it is important to provide support teachers with extrinsic rewards and incentives. Because funding is often required for extrinsic rewards, school districts and universities often neglect to include them. However, it is blatantly inappropriate to increase the responsibilities of veteran teachers who have the training and the ability to assume support teacher roles, without also rewarding them with tangible benefits. Rewards and incentives might include additional salary, release time from teaching, tuition waivers for university course work, and funding to travel to educational conferences. The form of the added benefits may not be as important as the fact that recognition is given for the substantial responsibilities being assumed. But rewards and incentives are essential because support teachers carry the major responsibility for passing the wisdom and the knowledge of accomplished teachers to the next generation of teachers.

Evaluating Programs

Although Chapter 5 deals extensively with the evaluation of beginning teacher assistance programs, not acknowledging here the importance of evaluation in the continuing development of such programs would be an oversight. Specifically it is important to engage in evaluation that continuously tracks the changing needs of the new teachers as they develop. Such evaluation permits the support offered to beginning teachers to be consonant with their need for assistance. Similarly the training offered to support teachers should be continuous, evaluating the skills and the content that they require to offer appropriate assistance to beginning teachers. Obviously the processes at work in effective programs are not static. It is through program evaluation that the dynamism involved in supporting beginners as they enter the teaching profession becomes manifest.

References

Bacharach, S. B., Bauer, G., & Shedd, J. (1986). *The learning workplace: The condition and resources of teaching.* Ithaca, NY: Organizational Analysis and Practice.

Burke, P., & Heideman, R. (Eds.). (1985). *Career-long teacher education.* Springfield, IL: Charles C. Thomas.

Burke, P., & Schmidt, W. (1984). Entry-year assistance: A promising practice. *Action in Teacher Education, 6,* 71–74.

Feiman-Nemser, S., Odell, S. J., & Lawrence, D. (1988). Induction programs and the professionalization of teachers: Two views. *Colloquy, 1*(2), 11–19.

Fox, S. M., & Singletary, T. J. (1986). Deductions about supportive induction. *Journal of Teacher Education, 37*(1), 12–15.

Fuller, F. F. (1969). Concerns of teachers: A developmental conceptualization. *American Educational Research Journal, 6,* 207–226.

Joyce, B. R., & Showers, B. (1982). The coaching of teaching. *Educational Leadership, 40,* 4–10.

Katz, L. G. (1972). Developmental stages of preschool teachers. *Elementary School Journal, 73,* 50–54.

Neuweiler, H. B. (1987). *Teacher education policy in the states: Fifty-state survey of legislative and administrative actions.* Washington, DC: American Association of Colleges for Teacher Education.

Odell, S. J. (1986a). Induction support of new teachers: A functional approach. *Journal of Teacher Education, 37*(1), 26–29.

Odell, S. J. (1986b). A model university–school system collaboration in teacher induction. *Kappa Delta Pi Record, 22,* 120–121.

Odell, S. J. (1987). *Stages of concern of beginning teachers in a collaborative internship induction program.* Paper presented at the annual meeting of the Association of Teacher Educators, Houston, TX.

Odell, S. J., Loughlin, C. E., & Ferraro, D. P. (1987). Functional approach to identification of new teacher needs in an induction context. *Action in Teacher Education, 8,* 51–57.

Schlechty, P., & Vance, V. (1983). Recruitment, selection and retention: The shape of the teaching force. *Elementary School Journal, 83,* 469–487.

Thies-Sprinthall, L. (1986). A collaborative approach for mentor training: A working model. *Journal of Teacher Education, 37*(6), 13–19.

Veenman, S. (1984). Perceived problems of beginning teachers. *Review of Educational Research, 54,* 143–178.

Watts, K. H. (1986). *How teachers learn: Teacher views on professional development.* Unpublished doctoral dissertation, Cornell University.

Additional Reading

Brooks, D. M. (Ed.). (1987). *Teacher induction: A new beginning.* Reston, VA: Association of Teacher Educators. (ERIC Document Reproduction Service No. 279 607).

Huffman, G., & Leak, S. (1986). Beginning teachers' perceptions of mentors. *Journal of Teacher Education, 37*(1), 22–25.

Stroble, E., & Cooper, J. M. (1988). Mentor teachers: Coaches or referees. *Theory into Practice, 27,* 231–236.

3

Research on Beginning Teacher Assistance Programs

Leslie Huling-Austin

As attention to programs that provide assistance to beginning teachers grows, a question being asked with increasing frequency is, What can be learned from research on the topic? Those asking want to know whether research data support the assumption that such programs make a difference.

Research on Assistance Programs in the Context of Program Goals

In a recent synthesis of research on assistance programs for beginning teachers (Huling-Austin, 1988), I used three criteria in selecting studies:

1. They had to be data based; that is, data had to have been systematically collected and analyzed.
2. They had to focus on beginning teachers (new to the profession) who had received some type of formal assistance.
3. They had to have been reported since 1977.

Studies were analyzed in terms of the five goals of beginning teacher assistance programs listed in Chapter 1:

1. To improve teaching performance
2. To increase the retention of promising beginning teachers
3. To promote the personal and the professional well-being of beginning teachers
4. To satisfy mandated requirements related to induction

5. To transmit the culture of the school system (and the teaching profession) to beginning teachers.

The purposes of beginning teacher assistance programs vary, but most have at least some of the above goals in mind. To facilitate access to the results of my synthesis, they are reported in relation to the five goals.

Goal 1: To Improve Teaching Performance

The idiosyncratic nature of teaching makes if difficult to measure teaching effectiveness or to compare the performance of one group of teachers with that of any other group of teachers. Even so, facilitators of programs to assist beginning teachers are beginning to tackle this issue and to document the effects of support and assistance on teaching performance.

Blackburn (1977) is the only researcher who has compared the achievement of students of first-year teachers who received assistance with the achievement of students of first-year teachers who did not receive assistance. He found no significant differences on this variable. However, he did find significant differences in how principals rated the teaching competence of the two groups of teachers. The teaching competence of teachers who had had cooperating teachers assigned to them on a one-to-one basis was rated significantly higher than that of nonsupported first-year teachers.

Summers (1987) reports outcomes for first-year teachers in Indiana State University's Project CREDIT (Certification Renewal Experiences Designed to Improve Teaching; see the appendix). He found that they showed specific and significant measurable changes when compared with a control group in (a) the use of mastery learning and mastery learning theory, (b) a motivation to understand and use higher-order questions, (c) inclination to teach critical thinking skills, (d) awareness of state and local curriculum guides, (e) ability to communicate with parents, and (f) ability to communicate with the public at large.

In an evaluation of the Oklahoma Entry-Year Assessment Program (Elsner, 1984), a sample of entry-year teachers, teacher consultants, school administrators, and higher education representatives was asked to rate the beginning teacher's knowledge, skills, and competencies in 10 areas at the beginning of the school year and again at the end. Data from this group of more than 200 respondents indicated that first-year teachers had made significant progress in developing planning skills, handling class discussions, preparing unit and lesson plans, managing discipline problems, and teaching or training others.

In an end-of-year study a colleague and I (Huling-Austin & Murphy, 1987) asked first-year teachers what changes they had made as a result of the assistance they had received through their beginning teacher program. Among the approximately 40 changes beginners reported were items such as these: "I've changed little things like voice inflection and eye contact," "I've changed my pacing; I was going too fast, especially through the transitions," and "[I've begun] to use different techniques like going from the chalkboard to the overhead in the same class." One of our conclusions was as follows:

It is interesting to note both the number and nature of the changes mentioned. The list indicates that a substantial amount of change is attributed by first-year teachers to the assistance they received through the induction program. Also, most of the changes are of an instructional nature and are of the type that directly influence the quality of instruction with students. (p. 23)

Using a similar approach for assessing improvement in teaching performance, Marockie and Looney (1988) measured beginning teachers' use of suggestions and recommendations acquired from their Teacher Induction Program (TIP). In written program evaluations the 15 beginning teachers in their study listed 20 ideas that they had used as a result of TIP: 67 percent of them reported making a better use of time in their instruction, and 33 percent reported that the program had prompted them to use praise, to conduct class "in a businesslike manner," to use better classroom management techniques, to use space more effectively, and to improve record keeping.

Teaching success is also influenced by placement. Beginning teachers are often given teaching assignments that would challenge even the most skillful veteran teachers. Such assignments can take several forms: teaching in a subject area for which the teacher is not certified; having too many class preparations; "floating" from classroom to classroom; working with low-ability, unmotivated, or disruptive students; or being responsible for demanding or time-consuming extracurricular activities.

Hidalgo (1986–87) recently completed a study of first-year emergency-credentialled teachers (beginners who had not completed preservice teacher preparation programs) in difficult settings. His case studies give vivid accounts of novice teachers assigned to teach high-demand subjects in low-income, overcrowded junior high schools while they were still enrolled in teacher preparation classes. Even less extreme circumstances can have major effects on beginners, according to a number of researchers who have studied the influence of assignment on beginning teacher success.

In a study of two state-mandated programs, Hoffman, Edwards, O'Neal, Barnes, and Paulissen (1986) found the following:

> The programs appeared to work best when the teaching context was appropriate to the talents and interests of the first-year teacher. The programs did not provide sufficient support to overcome inappropriate placements or stressful work conditions. And, in fact, in such situations the programs only served to further antagonize and exacerbate negative feelings. (p. 20)

In an earlier study (Huling-Austin, Putman, Edwards, & Galvez-Hjornevik, 1985), my colleagues and I came to a similar conclusion: "Placement of first-year teachers may well be the most influential variable in first-year teaching success. Which classes a first-year teacher is assigned to teach will be extremely influential in how successful a year that teacher is likely to have" (p. 48).

As a profession, teaching has a long way to go in being able to measure teaching performance with confidence. The problem is further compounded because it is unrealistic to use the same evaluation standards for beginning teachers as for experienced teachers. Beginning teacher assistance programs have only begun to address the ways in which and the degree to which they influence teaching performance. However, some progress has been made, and as improved evaluation measures, techniques, and instruments are developed specifically for use with beginning teachers, they will be incorporated into the overall evaluation designs of more programs.

Goal 2: To Increase the Retention of Promising Beginning Teachers

The literature documents well the fact that without support and assistance, many potentially good teachers become discouraged and abandon teaching careers (Ryan et al., 1980; Schlechty & Vance, 1983). Just how much beginning teacher assistance programs influence the retention of first-year teachers is not well documented, however. From the evidence available it appears that at least some programs help prevent beginners from leaving teaching. For example, after one year all 21 first-year teachers in Project CREDIT indicated a desire to return to teaching the following year. This compares with figures from a statewide needs assessment indicating that 26.5 percent of Indiana teachers who enter teaching drop out within two years (Summers, 1987).

Similarly impressive results have been reported by the University of Alabama/Birmingham First-Year Teacher Pilot Program (Blackburn, 1977). In this effort, data were collected from 100 first-year teachers receiving support and 100 first-year teachers not receiving support. Of the 100 teachers receiving support, only 4 did not teach the following year whereas 20 of the 100 without support did not teach the second year.

In fall 1983 Doane College in Nebraska instituted a beginning teacher support program as a part of teacher education. As of 1987, 24 of the 25 teachers who had completed the program remained in teaching; some were in their fourth year (Hegler & Dudley, 1987). Although it is difficult to know exactly the degree to which staying in teaching has been influenced by the support program, the 96 percent retention rate of Doane graduates suggests strongly that the program has had a positive influence on keeping new teachers in teaching.

Goal 3: To Promote the Personal and the Professional Well-Being of Beginning Teachers

Although all beginning teachers do not experience personal and professional trauma during their first-year even without support, many do. Hidalgo (1986–87), in studying emergency-credentialled teachers (those not prepared in regular teacher education programs) in the Los Angeles Unified School District found that teachers had persistent personal and management preoccupations that "obstructed, and even paralyzed their progress toward more sophisticated use of teaching knowledge" (p. 78). In several case studies he described in detail their anxieties, insecurities, and frustrations.

I contend that the profession has a responsibility for supporting the well-being of its members. Beginning teacher assistance programs provide one avenue for such support. A number of studies have reported positive outcomes in promoting well-being. One such study (Huffman & Leak, 1986) investigated the mentor teacher component of the North Carolina Initial Certification Program (see the appendix). "Mentor teachers were found to have provided 'positive reinforcement,' 'guidance and moral support,' 'patience and understanding,' and even 'a shoulder to cry on'" (p. 23). Studying beginning teachers in the Richardson (Texas) Intermediate School District program, Brooks (1986) found that assistance to beginning teachers resulted in increased feelings of competence, motivation, belonging, support, and attention as a result of experiences in the program.

A study of the Virginia Beginning Teacher Assistance Program produced evidence of the program's emotional contribution to beginning teachers' well-being (Wildman, Niles, Magliaro, McLaughlin, & Drill, 1987):

The chance to interact with a colleague by asking questions, sharing materials or planning collaboratively has other benefits of an emotional nature. The beginning teachers sense this support from the helping or nurturing attitudes of their colleagues and depend on it to get them through those first, difficult, lonely months. The beginning teachers report being comforted when the experienced teachers share their trials and frailties with them. (p. 12)

A colleague and I (Huling-Austin & Murphy, 1987) studied groups of beginning teachers across the country who were and were not participating in teacher induction programs. Using a questionnaire designed to measure the beginning teacher's own perception of his or her effectiveness and the desirability of the teaching profession, we found that "responses from sites that had no formal induction program in operation were noticeably less desirable than [responses from] the other sites" (p. 33). Summers (1987) found a similar situation in Project CREDIT. Comparisons with a control group revealed that intern teachers completed the year with significantly healthier attitudes and perceptions about teaching than did a similar group of beginning teachers who did not have the CREDIT support program. Nonsupported beginning teachers reported deteriorating attitudes or teaching perceptions on 88 of 98 surveyed variables. The findings from these two studies suggest that when beginning teachers are not supported, they may begin to question their own effectiveness and their decisions to become teachers.

Interestingly, although beginning teachers often report that the emotional support they receive is the most beneficial aspect of beginning teacher assistance, Odell (1986) has found in analyzing categories of support provided to first-year teachers that emotional support accounts for only a small percentage of the assistance provided. She concludes, "Although emotional support was of considerable importance across semesters, clinical support teachers generally offered more assistance with the formal teaching processes to new teachers than emotional support" (p. 28). This may suggest that without emotional support, beginning teachers have difficulty dealing with other matters, but once emotional support is established, they do not require large amounts of it and can move on rather quickly to deal with instructional matters.

Goal 4: To Satisfy Mandated Requirements Related to Induction

Once a mandated program is implemented, in a sense the mandate has been satisfied, but an important issue is the degree to which the original intent of the mandate is actually addressed. The following observations illustrate that some programs implementing mandates respond well to original intent but others do not.

Blackburn (1977), in his report on the University of Alabama/ Birmingham First-Year Teacher Pilot Program, notes, "Despite some program shortcomings, the project demonstrated that the local school systems, the State Department of Education, and institutions of higher education can work together and that the cooperative effort can result in a positive difference in the behavior of teachers" (p. 12).

Elsner (1984), in his evaluation of the first year of the Oklahoma Entry-Year Assistance Program, concludes as follows:

> For a new program with no model to follow the Entry-Year Assistance Program achieved an unusual number of their stated objectives. It appears that much of the apprehension expressed by some school administrators prior to program implementation had disappeared and that higher education faculty members made a significant contribution to the success of the program. Lines of communication have developed between teacher educators and practitioners in the field. (p. 7)

Friske and Combs (1986), who have also studied the Oklahoma Entry-Year Assistance Program, report that the program by and large has been implemented across the state. Their concern, however, is that studies of the program have focused on the ways in which the program has been implemented and the factors influencing implementation, and have not examined the extent to which the program has fulfilled the original intent of "improving the quality of teaching in Oklahoma" (p. 72).

A comparable concern has been expressed by another set of researchers reporting on their study of two state-mandated programs (Hoffman, Edwards, O'Neal, Barnes, & Paulissen, 1986):

At the school level, our analyses of implementation focused on the work of the support teams with the beginning teacher. It is useful to draw a distinction at this level between procedural compliance and substantive implementation of program requirements. Procedurally, the teams included in our sample accomplished all of the required activities in terms of observing, conferring, completing necessary forms, and so on. Substantively there was great variance in terms of how the program was carried out. . . . In cases where no strong team leadership appeared, the induction program seldom rose above the procedural compliance level. (p. 19)

These same researchers also take note of an interesting point on the gatekeeping function of beginning teacher programs. Data secured from interviews with state officials in the two states revealed that nearly all of the teachers in the state who had been enrolled in the two state programs were recommended for certification. Their comment: "Such patterns would seem to call into question either the 'gate-keeping' capacity of such programs or the real need for such programs in the first place on the grounds of controlling for the quality of entering teachers" (Hoffman, Edwards, O'Neal, Barnes, & Paulissen, 1986, p. 18).

Goal 5: To Transmit the Culture of the System (and the Profession) to Beginning Teachers

This goal appears to be less deliberate in many programs than the other four. Although many programs recognize that one function is to "socialize" beginning teachers and familiarize them with workplace norms, most programs stop far short of defining and transmitting the culture of the system. Almost none, as yet, attempt to transmit the professional culture of teaching.

One can speculate that locally developed programs emphasize the culture goal more often than state-mandated programs do because local agencies are more likely to "own" a common culture that they want to transmit to the beginning teacher. The two studies that address this goal most directly focused on locally developed programs.

The Ohio County Schools Teacher Induction Program in Wheeling, West Virginia, has as one of its objectives that teachers develop a sense of ownership and bonding to the school system (Marockie & Looney, 1988). Researchers evaluating the program indicate that it—

> was extremely successful in guiding inductees in becoming bonded to the system and adopting the goals of the system. Through a positive interaction between central office personnel and new teacher as well as principal and new teacher, ownership began to develop. Results seem to suggest that each teacher became more and more a part of the system and the sense of belonging to an excellent system became greater and greater. Out of the developing ownership emerged a real commitment to the system and the teacher's role in it. (pp. 2–3)

A similar phenomenon is described by Brooks (1986) in his analysis of the Richardson (Texas) Intermediate School District beginning teacher program. He concludes, "Beginning teacher reports of increased feelings of competence, motivation, belonging, support, and attention combine to produce an overwhelming perception of district competence and motivation to assist and develop entry-year professionals" (p. 7). From Brooks's observation it can be inferred that the Richardson program has addressed the goal of transmitting the culture of the district to beginning teachers and has accomplished it to a reasonably high degree.

Developers and implementors of beginning teacher assistance programs have not yet given much thought to transmitting the culture of the system to the new teacher. As more programs incorporate this goal and researchers report results, greater numbers of those working in the field may begin to recognize the benefits of such a goal and address it more directly.

A caution is in order. When programs are deliberate in achieving this goal, there should be careful consideration of the difference between orientation and indoctrination, and clear recognition that school culture, positive or negative, good or bad, is transmitted to every beginning teacher—directly or indirectly, whether or not there is a beginning teacher assistance program. The very process of transmitting a school district or professional culture may provide an opportunity to examine that culture and perhaps to do something about it if it needs improvement.

Implications of Research Findings for Beginning Teacher Assistance Programs

These studies have a number of specific implications for program development. For example, they suggest that the existence of a beginning teacher assistance program influences how teachers perceive their own effectiveness and the desirability of the teaching profession. First-year teachers report making a large number of changes in their teaching as a result of the assistance they receive. Therefore, the first implication is that it is in the school district's best interest to have a beginning teacher assistance program. A couple of hypotheses seem apparent:

1. The existence of such programs helps teachers (and others) realize that beginners are not expected to be polished professionals their first week or month (or even year) on the job.
2. It is acceptable, even desirable, to seek help with teaching, particularly in the beginning years.

These hypotheses are supported by data indicating that the least desirable responses to assistance and the least general satisfaction with teaching come from beginning teachers who receive no formal or deliberate support. To state it another way, the very existence of a program to assist beginners appears to make a difference in how first-year teachers perceive their own teaching and the teaching profession.

Another implication from these studies is that assigning a support teacher to a novice may well be the most powerful and most cost-effective induction practice available to program developers. First-year teachers consistently report that they rely most heavily for assistance on the support teacher to whom they are assigned. When there is no designated support teacher, first-year teachers either "work it out on their own" or rely on "the teacher across the hall" or some other receptive teacher at the school. Implications for the development of support teachers are as follows:

- They should receive training in how to fulfill their role, including how to work with another adult in a supportive fashion.
- The district's expectations of them should be made clear to help them balance their desire to be helpful against their desire not to be perceived as interfering.
- They should be compensated for their work with beginning teachers because data indicate that the role is substantial. Districts should reward them with money, released time, and other forms of professional recognition.

Another set of implications for program development relates to how educators and the public view beginning teacher assistance programs. The program should be considered the entry piece of a larger, continuing staff development program for teachers. Learning to teach is not a one-year process, and it is doubtful whether any program can ever be so strong that it transforms beginning teachers into polished professionals in one year.

District administrators should also have realistic expectations for beginning teacher assistance programs. Programs will seldom, if ever, be powerful enough to overcome the difficulties that beginning teachers experience when placed in an extremely difficult teaching context. A variety of factors can contribute to a difficult context, such as being assigned classes predominantly composed of low-achieving students who are unmotivated to learn; having an extremely high student-teacher ratio; being responsible for a large number of preparations; and carrying heavy extracurricular responsibilities. It is estimated that more than 12 percent of all newly hired teachers are not certified in the field to which they are assigned (Roth, 1986). A beginning teacher support program should not be expected to overcome the influence of misassignments and overloads.

Needed Next Steps in Research

Progress has been made in research on the beginning teacher in the past few years, yet many questions remain. A number of educators have identified avenues to be explored through further research: Griffin (1985) provides a lengthy list of stimulating research questions and pressing research issues; McCaleb (1985) points out the need to investigate the effects of specific induction interventions as well as the cumulative effects of specific beginning teacher programs; and Zeichner (1982) argues that there is a critical need to investigate the influence of specific contexts in which beginning teachers function. Collectively these recommendations are extremely valuable in determining direction and focus for future research efforts on the beginning year(s) of teaching.

Teacher educators have reached a point in research on the beginning teacher at which they can turn their attention to answering the question, What practices work best under what conditions? (Huling-Austin,1987). Although important progress has been made in documenting the effects of beginning teacher assistance programs in a number of areas (Huling-Austin, 1988), research is still not at all clear about what specific practices or what combination of them is achieving what outcomes.

To determine this, it is necessary to undertake several kinds of efforts in addition to investigating the effects of beginning teacher programs. Teacher educators must do a much better job of documenting the particular components and practices included in programs, as well as the contexts in which programs operate. Then they should compare effects across similar and different programs and contexts. The degree to which legislative mandates are achieving their original intent is also extremely important to investigate. The difficult task of determining what works requires careful attention on the part of researchers studying specific programs as well as a concerted effort by other researchers to tackle the task of analyzing and synthesizing findings across studies. It is also important to be aware of the danger of trying to export a program that works well in one setting to other settings that may have completely different constraints and demands.

The most intriguing questions, yet the most difficult to answer, are these:

1. To what degree do beginning teacher assistance programs change teachers' attitudes about professional development and the desirability of the teaching profession?
2. What are the long-range effects of attitude changes on (a) teacher retention, (b) teacher effectiveness, and (c) efforts to recruit new talent into teaching?

One can speculate that if a beginning teacher's first experience with on-the-job professional development is highly effective and rewarding, that teacher will have a positive attitude about other professional development opportunities. If such a teacher approaches future professional development with a more open mind, his or her performance is more likely to improve as a result of that experience than is the performance of a teacher who has a poor attitude. A beginning teacher who experiences a meaningful and systematic induction into the profession will probably view the profession more positively and judge his or her own decision to enter the profession as a good one. Such a person is also more likely to encourage others to enter the profession.

Whatever directions are explored in research on programs of assistance to beginning teachers, it is important that multiple questions be asked and appropriate methodologies be used to answer them. Griffin (1985) makes the point well:

> To understand the interactions around and within complex contexts such as schools, I believe it is absolutely necessary that we make much more vigorous use of methodologies that blend and explain, that answer and provide needed detail, and that name and describe. This blend is only possible when complementary although basically different conceptions of scientific inquiry can be used in tandem. (p. 45)

Finally, as the body of research on beginning teacher assistance programs grows, there is an increasing need for researchers to translate their findings into formats that are useful to policy makers and practitioners, and to develop improved strategies for communicating these findings.

Summary

As this synthesis reflects, there are research data to support the existence of beginning teacher assistance programs, and there is evidence to suggest that such programs can successfully achieve the goals outlined earlier. However, those developing and implementing programs must realize that to achieve goals to any appreciable degree, program features and activities must be targeted to specific goals. Program facilitators can make their own decisions about which goals to emphasize and to what degree, but they should recognize that goals are rarely achieved by accident just because a program exists.

Finally, if the art and the science of inducting new teachers into the profession is to advance, teacher educators must continue to push the boundaries of their knowledge and to recognize that learning to teach is a lifelong process spanning preservice preparation, induction, and inservice practice. Policy makers, practitioners, and researchers must continue to work together to provide better programs for inducting new teachers into the profession.

References

Blackburn, J. (1977). *The first-year teacher: Perceived needs, intervention strategies and results.* Paper presented at the annual meeting of the American Educational Research Association, New York. (ERIC Document Reproduction Service No. ED 135 768).

Brooks, D. M. (1986). *Richardson new teacher induction program: Final data analysis and report.* Richardson, TX: Richardson Intermediate School District. (ERIC Document Reproduction Service No. ED 278 627).

Elsner, K. (1984). *First-year evaluation results from Oklahoma's Entry-Year Assistance Committees.* Paper presented at the annual meeting of the Association of Teacher Educators, New Orleans. (ERIC Document Reproduction Service No. 242 706).

Friske, J., & Combs, M. (1986). Teacher induction programs: An Oklahoma perspective. *Action in Teacher Education, 7,* 67–74.

Griffin, G. A. (1985). Teacher induction: Research issues. *Journal of Teacher Education, 36*(1), 42–46.

Hegler, K., & Dudley, R. (1987). Beginning teacher induction: A progress report. *Journal of Teacher Education, 38*(1), 53–56.

Hidalgo, F. (1986–87). The evolving concerns of first-year junior high school teachers in difficult settings: Three case studies. *Action in Teacher Education, 8,* 75–79.

Hoffman, J. V., Edwards, S. A., O'Neal, S., Barnes, S., & Paulissen, M. (1986). A study of state-mandated beginning teacher programs. *Journal of Teacher Education, 37*(1), 16–21.

Huffman, G., & Leak, S. (1986). Beginning teachers' perceptions of mentors. *Journal of Teacher Education, 37*(1), 22–25.

Huling-Austin, L. (1987). Teacher induction. In D. M. Brooks (Ed.), *Teacher induction: A new beginning* (pp. 3–24). Reston, VA: Association of Teacher Educators.

Huling-Austin, L. (1988). *A synthesis of research on teacher induction programs and practices.* Paper presented at the annual meeting of the American Educational Research Association, New Orleans.

Huling-Austin, L., & Murphy, S. C. (1987). *Assessing the impact of teacher induction programs: Implications for program development.* Paper presented at the annual meeting of the American Educational Research Association, Washington, DC. (ERIC Document Reproduction Service No. 283 779).

Huling-Austin, L., Putman, S., Edwards, S., & Galvez-Hjornevik, C. (1985). *MTIP Satellite Conference proceedings* (Report No. 7209). Austin, TX: University of Texas at Austin, Research and Development Center for Teacher Education.

Marockie, M., & Looney, G. E. (1988). *Evaluating teacher induction in Ohio County Schools, Wheeling, West Virginia.* Paper presented at the annual meeting of the Association of Teacher Educators, San Diego.

McCaleb, J. L. (1985). *Summary of research on induction.* Paper presented at the Forum of Teacher Education, Virginia Beach, VA.

Odell, S. J. (1986). Induction support of new teachers: A functional approach. *Journal of Teacher Education, 37*(1), 26–29.

Roth, R. A. (1986). Emergency certificates, misassignments of teachers, and other "dirty little secrets." *Phi Delta Kappan, 67*, 725–727.

Ryan, K., Newman, K., Mager, G., Applegate, J., Lasley, T., Flora, R., & Johnston, J. (1980). *Biting the apple: Accounts of first-year teachers.* New York: Longman.

Schlechty, P., & Vance, V. (1983). Recruitment, selection and retention: The shape of the teaching force. *Elementary School Journal, 83*, 469–487.

Summers, J. A. (1987). *Summative evaluation report: Project CREDIT.* Terre Haute, IN: Indiana State University, School of Education.

Wildman, T. M., Niles, J. A., Magliaro, S. G., McLaughlin, R. A., & Drill, L. G. (1987). *Virginia's colleague teacher project: Focus on beginning teachers' adaptation to teaching.* Paper presented at the annual meeting of the American Educational Research Association, Washington, DC.

Zeichner, K. (1982). *Why bother with induction?* Paper presented at the annual meeting of the American Educational Research Association, New York.

Additional Reading

Butler, E. D. (1987). *Lessons learned about mentoring in two fifth-year teacher preparation-induction programs.* Memphis, TN: Memphis State University, Center of Excellence in Teacher Education.

Kilgore, A. M., & Kozisek, J. A. (1988). *The effects of a planned induction program on first-year teachers: A research report.* Paper presented at the annual meeting of the Association of Teacher Educators, San Diego.

-4

Impact of Beginning Teacher Assistance Programs

Peggy Ishler and Roy A. Edelfelt

To provide a perspective on the impact of programs to assist the beginning teacher, this chapter examines information from 17 of them that were showcased at a leadership academy in June 1988 cosponsored by the Association of Teacher Educators and Rhode Island College. The 17 are described more fully in the appendix, in alphabetical order by state and project name. Here we explore their effects on beginning teachers, support teachers, schools, teacher education programs in colleges and universities, and activities at the state level. The analysis builds on the data presented in Chapter 3 and draws on a few sources in addition to the program descriptions, including supplementary information provided by program personnel and a review of the literature by the Maryland Department of Education and Research for Better Schools (1987) .

Impact on Beginning Teachers

Retention

A large percentage of all beginning teachers leave the profession within the first three years (Schlechty & Vance, 1983). For that reason we examine first whether receiving help in the initial year(s) influences beginners to remain in teaching.

The Florida Beginning Teacher Program provides support during the first year of employment. Statewide in 1986–87, 4,721 novice teachers successfully completed the program (P. Cheavers, personal communication, March 1989). Beginners are assisted by a support team, which includes a peer teacher, a school administrator (usually the principal), and another professional educator (usually a district-level supervisor or a higher education person). The program also includes assessment of the minimum generic competencies required by the state, but only the administrator evaluates for job retention or certification. The Florida program, then, serves as both an assistance program and a screening device for entry into the profession.

In Project CREDIT (Certification Renewal Experiences Designed to Improve Teaching), developed by the Department of Secondary Education at Indiana State University (Terre Haute) and 10 school districts in west-central Indiana, all 20 interns from the first year of the program (1987) remained in teaching the second year. This ratio is impressive when one considers that 26.5 percent of beginning teachers in Indiana drop out of teaching within the first two years (Summers, 1987).

The Teacher Induction Program in Albuquerque, New Mexico, which is collaboratively operated by the local public school system and the University of New Mexico, serves all beginning teachers in the system. The program director reports that 86 percent of the graduates from 1984 and 1985 were still teaching four years after entry into the profession (Odell, 1988).

In the Teacher Induction Program of the Ohio County Schools, Wheeling, West Virginia, as of May 1987, 68 of the 73 beginning teachers who had participated since the program's formation in 1979 were continuing in their teaching positions in the county. An evaluation indicates that the program, which involves a three-year skill development approach and includes support teacher supervisors in subject-matter areas, has been extremely successful in bonding beginning teachers to the system (Marockie & Marockie, 1988).

More programs should be encouraged to study retention. The scarcity of data leaves one wondering whether there is under-reporting or whether the contribution of beginning teacher assistance programs to holding power is being given sufficient attention.

Support for Well-Being

A second important purpose of assistance programs is to promote the well-being of the novice teacher, that is, to provide personal, emotional support as well as instructional aid. All of the programs in our sample arrange for support teachers or assistance teams to work closely with beginners during the difficult first year to help them succeed.

The New Teacher Support Project of Oakland School District and California State University at Hayward focuses on helping beginning inner-city teachers learn how to overcome the difficulties of urban teaching. The program seeks to combat the isolation of novices and to provide them with support in addressing crises through immediate, continuing personal contact with a support teacher, as well as through access to a trained teacher consultant during the first year. The project demonstrates that teachers can be successful and can have rewarding careers despite the difficulties inherent in inner-city teaching (Waters & Watson, 1988).

The Intern-Mentor Program in the District of Columbia Public Schools has been structured so that novices can bring difficult experiences from their classrooms to problem-solving sessions with professors of education and veteran teachers. They are thus helped to cope with their problems.

Intern teachers in Indiana State University's Project CREDIT completed the first year with significantly healthier attitudes and perceptions about teaching than did a similar group of beginners who were not in the project (Henry, 1988). Project CREDIT uses a system of multiple supports that includes an experienced teacher, a university supervisor, and university consultants.

Four years after graduation, teachers in Albuquerque, New Mexico's Teacher Induction Program reported that it had greatly enhanced their self-confidence (S. J. Odell, personal communication, March 1989).

In Teachers Need Teachers, the Chesterfield County (Va.) Mentor Teacher Program, beginning teachers receive emotional support as well as instructional aid from support teachers. They report that having someone to whom they can direct questions, with whom they can share problems, and from whom they can receive helpful feedback and reinforcement is very beneficial, particularly in the first months when they are the most insecure (Wildman & Magliaro, 1988).

Improvement of Teaching Performance

A third purpose of assistance programs is to help beginners improve their teaching. This purpose is present in all of the programs that were examined. The ways used to achieve this goal vary from courses for credit, such as those offered in the university-centered induction model of the Wisconsin Department of Public Instruction, to videotaping and feedback sessions with support teachers in a number of other programs. Improving teacher performance by observing teachers other than the support teacher is used in the Indiana Department of Education's (1988) Beginning Teacher Internship Program (not included in our sample).

In Indiana State University's Project CREDIT, a follow-up research study (Summers, 1987) revealed that interns demonstrated greater use of mastery learning, increased use of higher-order questions, more awareness of state and local curriculum guides, enhanced ability to communicate with parents, and improved ability to communicate with the public.

The University of New Hampshire has a five-year teacher education program in which the last year is an internship. The intern is essentially a beginning teacher, but is supervised by a university professor and a public school teacher. The program places induction at the end of formal preparation rather than at the beginning of employment. University professors report that when their graduates take jobs after the internship, they begin with the maturity of second- or third-year teachers (J. Krull, personal communication, March 1989).

In none of the 17 programs that were examined has there been an attempt to compare the achievement of students in the classes of beginning teachers receiving assistance with the achievement of students in the classes of first-year teachers not receiving help. In Chapter 3, Huling-Austin cites only one such investigation (Blackburn, 1977). This is an area for future study.

Only a few programs emphasize the importance of helping teachers engage in self-evaluation and reflect on their teaching. A pioneer in this approach, not included in our sample, is the Franklin County–Ohio State University Induction Project (1988), which has placed major emphasis on working with beginners to become "reflective" professionals. Albuquerque, New Mexico's Teacher Induction Program focuses on self-analysis by incorporating coaching into the program. The primary goal is to stimulate beginners to analyze their own teaching. Ohio County, West Virginia's Teacher Induction Program endeavors to develop self-analysis through videotaping. The Teachers Need Teachers program in Chesterfield County, Virginia, encourages teachers to see themselves as reflective practitioners.

The limited attention in our sample to developing reflective and self-evaluative skills may be a lack of reporting. We encourage more coverage in those programs in which reflection is promoted, and in those in which it is not, we advocate more thought and attention to such introspection by both teacher educators and public school instructional leaders. If teachers are to improve their skills beyond the entry year, in which they may receive considerable feedback through an assistance program, they need to learn the tools of analysis and reflection so that they can become self-monitors and continue to grow.

Impact on Support Teachers

Increased Professional Growth and Satisfaction

All of the programs except one use support teachers or support teams. Support teachers are recognized as key people in every beginning teacher program. Among those using support teams are California State University at Chico's Induction for the Beginning Teacher program; Broward County, Florida's Beginning Teacher Program; the mentoring programs of Nash and Wake counties in North Carolina; and Memphis (Tenn.) State University's MAT Internship Program.

Every program director in the projects that were reviewed testifies that support teachers report considerable professional growth as a result of their training and work with beginning teachers. Also, they feel increased pride in the profession and in their own competence.

Increased Knowledge About Teaching and Assisting Beginners

Fifteen of the 17 programs in the sample require training for support teachers. Support teachers credit their training with giving them considerable information on teaching and the support role. In the mentoring program of Nash County, North Carolina, training in North Carolina Effective Teaching and North Carolina Performance Appraisal is a prerequisite for the support teacher role. In the mentoring program of Wake County, North Carolina, a "state-of-the-art" two-semester intensive training program is required of teachers supervising either student or beginning teachers. Support teachers learn how to build a helping relationship, employ effective teaching skills, use developmental supervision strategies, and employ cognitive developmental matches. A Wake County elementary school teacher who completed the training testified, "The personal growth that took place was the most significant experience in the course for me. I am much more tuned in to specific teaching skills that I was beginning to put 'on the back burner.' I feel that I am a more effective teacher because of this course."

The amount of training for support teachers varies across the 17 programs included in our sample. The New Teacher Support Project of Oakland and California State University at Hayward trains support teachers and consultants in elements of cognitive coaching in a session lasting two days. In the Teacher Induction Program of Albuquerque, New Mexico, support teachers receive a week of intensive preparation before the school year begins and then participate in weekly four-hour training sessions. North Carolina requires 24 hours statewide; a two-semester program is an option in some school districts. Wisconsin's university-centered induction model calls for the first-year teacher and the support teacher to take a three-credit-hour course. In Indiana's Beginning Teacher Internship Program, not included in our sample, there is a stipulation of training for both support teachers and principals, the extent of it to be determined by each school corporation (Indiana Department of Education, 1988).

The quantity and the quality of training for support teachers in the sample vary considerably, but preparing personnel to work with beginning teachers is recognized as an essential part of any effective assistance program. Being an accomplished teacher is not preparation enough because more than teaching competence is required. Support teachers need competence in coaching and working with adult teachers, skill in analyzing teaching, a broad knowledge of teaching materials, special skills in curriculum development, know-how in advising and conferring, and empathy as listeners. These skills must be taught, and they are difficult to teach and to learn. Also, teaching them requires a considerable budget. Much of the training that was reported appears to be done minimally and only in some programs.

Impact on Schools

Interactive Effects with Context or Environment

The context in which a beginning teacher is placed has a major influence on his or her success. By *context* we mean all the factors that make up the environment and the circumstance in which the teacher works, including the type and the number of students, the teaching assignment in subject and level, the number of preparations, the size and the nature of the faculty, the physical work space, the social and psychological climate, the support staff available, the quality of leadership by the principal, etc. All these (and more) influence the possible effectiveness of the beginning teacher, whether or not he or she is given assistance in the first year of teaching. Research (Huling-Austin, 1988) indicates that attention to the factors of context will reduce teaching difficulties.

Several approaches are used to help beginners orient and cope with context, but only a few of the programs surveyed give attention to contextual considerations. Personnel in Oakland–California State University at Hayward's New Teacher Support Project are sensitive to creating a supportive teaching environment for beginners in inner-city schools. The main focus is the work of the school principal in helping to provide an environment conducive to teacher success. The Wake County, North Carolina, mentoring program strives to give beginners a realistic work load, with special attention to the number and the types of classes assigned. In the Wisconsin residency model, a first-year teacher is assigned a lighter teaching load and receives two-thirds the salary of a regular first-year teacher. However, first-year teachers carry 12 graduate credits. This hardly represents a reduction in overall responsibility.

The relative lack of attention to context raises the question of whether environmental factors are perceived as important to the success of the beginning teacher. The factors are numerous and often subtle. It is common knowledge that teaching is made more difficult by having large classes, teaching in a field for which one is not prepared, being assigned the more difficult students, having multiple preparations, and lacking curriculum materials. In addition, variables such as low socioeconomic status and poor English-language facility among students, many mainstreamed students, inadequate numbers of special service personnel, poor school climate, and inept leadership can cause major problems for beginning teachers. The need to consider context is among the most critical in giving beginning teachers a fair chance for success.

Changes in Inservice Education and Professional Development

Attending to the special needs of the beginning teacher has required differentiated inservice education programs in school districts across the country. Some of the programs in our sample illustrate different ways of responding to the varying needs. The Beginning Teacher Program in Broward County, Florida, involves separate components for inexperienced teachers, experienced teachers, and candidates for alternative certification. In Chesterfield County, Virginia's Teachers Need Teachers program, novice teachers are individually assisted by support teachers. The program includes meetings in both formal and informal settings, release days, needs assessment through bimonthly "temperature checks" by support teachers, and individual or small group sessions to address needs.

The developmental nature of improving and refining teaching as a lifelong process seems to be evident in many programs. Using the developmental literature to help design appropriate programs for beginning teachers and support teachers illustrates one way in which school districts are demonstrating a greater sense of obligation to the professional development of all their teachers. This commitment is articulated in the New Teacher Support Project of Oakland–California State University at Hayward, in which a program goal is to encourage a positive attitude toward continuing professional development among beginning inner-city teachers. A feeling of empowerment is cultivated in the professional development of new teachers by helping them learn to enhance their resource networks. Beginning teachers design their own professional development contract (with the district) to guide them through the activities and released time of their induction program. A second-year, follow-up component is included in the plan. It enables second-year teachers to receive release days for professional development activities, and it continues the beginner-veteran team. All beginning teachers, including second-year ones, must complete a contract that specifies the ways in which they will identify goals for professional improvement and the strategies that they will use to reach those goals.

The mentoring program in Wake County, North Carolina, links assistance to the beginning teacher to the total staff development program, thus expressing a commitment to long-term professional development. Support teachers are prepared in a two-semester sequence that covers the theory and the practice of supervision and coaching, followed by a practicum in which teachers work with student teachers, beginning teachers, and colleagues. The training is conducted by classroom teachers prepared in a three-semester university sequence that includes serving as a support teacher.

A developmental model at the preservice level, incorporating a phased internship, is the center of the MAT Internship Program at Memphis State University in Tennessee. The program features an integrative approach to teacher preparation with a year-long internship (in the fifth year) that involves candidates in nearly every role that first-year teachers experience, but under supervised, benign conditions. A support teacher team is assigned to interns. Beginning teachers are allowed to undergo the local school system evaluation for initial licensure at the apprentice level rather than at the probationary level, which is the typical license for beginning teachers. Beginners report less stress as a result of contextual factors in schools after completing the preservice program.

The Teacher Induction Program of West Virginia's Ohio County Schools entails a three-year developmental induction that builds a strong collegial network, disseminates up-to-date information about the system, and builds positive system allies. The program emphasizes the transmission of the culture of the school system.

Career-Ladder Opportunities

School systems are beginning to recognize that working as support teachers in programs for beginning teachers provides career-ladder opportunities for successful, experienced professionals. Master teachers, as part of their career-ladder designation, can play an important role in serving as support teachers and as trainers of support teachers without adding substantially to a district's costs for assistance programs. In the Induction for the Beginning Teacher program of California State University at Chico, peer coaches can earn three graduate credits that can be used to meet requirements for the second tier of an administrative credential. Some North Carolina systems require teachers to be above the first step in a career ladder to be eligible for the support teacher role. In the Teachers Need Teachers program of Chesterfield County, Virginia, support teachers are trained by teams of "super mentors" who are classroom teachers with two previous years of mentoring experience on an assistance team.

A concern in many programs is that support teachers not be considered supervisors, that is, that they not be a part of the administrative structure of the school. (*Supervisors* here refers to personnel who evaluate teachers for employment and tenure.)

The Indiana Department of Education's (1988) Beginning Teacher Internship Program (not included in our sample) emphasizes this point by prohibiting support teachers from becoming supervisors as a result of their work in beginning teacher programs.

Financial Impact

Another aspect of impact is cost. Training and releasing support and beginning teachers, stipends for mentors, and other program features require time and money. Some schools receive funding from their state legislatures; others depend on the contributions of several public agencies; still others must rely entirely on their own school districts for financing. More than money is included in the term *contributions.*

State governments that allocate monies for beginning teacher programs include those in California, the District of Columbia, Florida, Georgia, Indiana, North Carolina, Tennessee, Virginia, Washington, and Wisconsin. Several programs in our sample are funded by grants resulting from proposals developed jointly by a university, school districts, and the state department of education. A few programs are funded exclusively by a district or a county—for example, the Teacher Induction Program of Ohio County, West Virginia. The Teacher Induction Program in Albuquerque, New Mexico, which functions in elementary schools, is advertised as operating at "no additional cost." Regular teachers are released to serve full-time as clinical support teachers, and fully certified graduate interns take their places. Interns gain a year's teaching experience and pursue a master's degree through a fellowship from the University of New Mexico, which includes tuition waivers for two semesters and two summers. Support teachers maintain their full salary and benefits as teachers, are trained in assisting beginning teachers, and have a chance to view teaching and the profession more broadly.

Earmarking funds in the school budget for programs to assist beginning teachers is not yet a common practice around the country. Policy makers must be convinced that beginning teacher assistance programs are necessary. The most equitable system for all school districts is state support through additional funding.

Impact on Teacher Education

Providing the beginner with special assistance in the first year of teaching establishes a transition between preparation and practice. It creates an induction phase and takes some of the pressure off teacher education institutions, in recognition that preparing a beginner to be fully functional upon graduation from college is seldom feasible. Teachers, like other professionals, need an induction period, a time between being a college student and assuming full status as a practitioner, when they can work into their professional role gradually. Educators and policy makers, through the work being done with first-year teachers, are beginning to acknowledge that developing a professional takes many years. It requires not only special attention in the beginning years, but also professional development for an entire career.

Programs to assist beginning teachers appear to be increasing collaboration between schools and teacher education institutions. In the 17 programs that were examined, there is more shared responsibility for teacher education (preservice and inservice) than before, more precise identification of competencies required of beginning teachers in the preservice curriculum, and more feedback to colleges of education on whether new teachers are adequately prepared to begin teaching. Concern for the initial year of teaching has also encouraged the development of creative fifth-year internship programs and alternative routes to certification.

Increased Collaboration

Fifteen of the 17 programs in our sample employ a collaborative approach to induction that includes higher education institutions, local education agencies, and sometimes state departments of education. Of the remaining two, one program is controlled and delivered by a county district, the other by a college of education.

Collaboration takes many forms. At some institutions of higher education, faculty train support teachers and beginning teachers on campus; at other colleges, professors serve on support teams for beginning teachers; at still others, staff provide training for local district personnel to assist beginning teachers.

An example of the expansive nature of collaboration is the Arizona Teacher Residency Project, funded by the Arizona Department of Education. It unites Northern Arizona University and Arizona State University with over 60 school districts in partnerships that cover the state. The universities provide training to support teachers, resident teachers, and cooperating teachers. The collaboration includes gathering evaluative feedback on the degree to which beginning teachers achieve essential competencies and communicating the results back to the universities.

The Arizona Teacher Residency Project illustrates how collaboration in three separate residency projects coalesces preservice and inservice needs of teachers and provides data for assessing the effectiveness of preservice programs. An observation instrument, which specifies 30 measurable teacher competencies, is used to document skill development of both student teachers and beginning teachers. The observation data supply feedback to the teacher education programs, and they are also used by the schools to identify staff development needs.

Another collaborative project is the Teacher Induction Program of the Albuquerque Public Schools and the University of New Mexico, through which all beginning teachers in the system's 76 elementary and 34 secondary schools receive support. The system releases 24 veteran teachers, 17 elementary school and 7 secondary school, to provide support to both preservice and beginning teachers. In exchange, the university provides 28 elementary school and 18 secondary school graduate interns to serve as first-year teachers. All program personnel are selected jointly, program planning and evaluation are accomplished in the partnership, and the program director's salary is paid jointly by the university and the school system.

Identification of Generic Teaching Competencies

In some states an assessment instrument specifies the teaching competencies to be taught in their preservice teacher education programs and to be evaluated in an internship or probationary period. Obviously such an instrument has considerable impact in standardizing the focus of teacher education. Florida, Georgia, Indiana, and North Carolina are among the states that require the use of a state assessment instrument. Beginning teachers must be evaluated and rated satisfactory using the state instrument before being granted certification. These four states include competency assessment as part of an assistance program. The Florida Beginning Teacher Program has identified 35 generic competencies that are required to be taught in state-approved programs of teacher education. Beginning teachers must successfully demonstrate competence in these 35 areas in order to receive initial certification.

The use of state assessment instruments raises the question of the wisdom of combining assistance and assessment in beginning teacher programs. It also prompts concern about the identification of one set of competencies for all teachers, regardless of the teacher's role, and the standardization of certain teaching behaviors, irrespective of individual styles and varying teaching contexts.

Curriculum Revision

Beginning teacher assistance programs serve as a vehicle for teacher education reform by providing feedback on the operational capabilities of recent graduates. When teacher educators and other higher education faculty work with beginners and support teachers, data become available for continuous program development and revision. Faculty can observe beginning teachers firsthand and discover whether the college program has done a good job of preparing students to begin teaching.

The Arizona Teacher Residency Project includes research on the acquisition of teaching skills, to be used in the refinement of preservice and residency programs. Observation data gathered through the program are fed back to preservice program personnel to assist them in revision and development.

The Oakland–California State University at Hayward New Teacher Support Project, for example, provides an opportunity for education professors to examine the preservice teacher education program in light of the adequacy of their graduates on entering the profession. Through their work as academic resource consultants, faculty across the campus translate their content into forms appropriate at the elementary and secondary levels, to be used as curriculum resources in courses frequently taken by undergraduates planning to become teachers.

In the Teacher Induction Program of Albuquerque, support teachers meet with University of New Mexico faculty to discuss the strengths and the weaknesses of new teachers in the Albuquerque system who have graduated from the university. Names are kept confidential, in the interest of the general effectiveness of the preservice program.

Alternative Approaches to Beginning Teacher Assistance Programs

Alternative approaches to traditional teacher education have had an impact on beginning teacher assistance programs. However, the nature of that impact depends on whether the alternative is a fifth-year program or some other route to certification. Fifth-year programs of various sorts have been offered by some institutions for the last 40 years, but the idea has been refined and become more attractive with the requirement in some states and institutions of an internship or residency. The University of New Hampshire offers a five-year teacher education program featuring a full-year internship in the fifth year (after college course work in education) that includes graduate work leading to a master's degree. The internship is credited by most districts as a full year of teaching. Interns are assigned a university supervisor and a classroom teacher to work with them throughout the year. The program provides a guided transition between study and practice under the auspices of the university. Internships do not constitute first-year employment in the usual sense, although they may offer an entree to a job when a vacancy is available.

A controversial development in teacher education is the so-called alternative certification route. The approach takes several forms. The most popular one allows a liberal arts graduate to begin teaching with little or no professional education and to be supervised on the job while taking graduate work that includes education courses, all of which lead to certification.

Georgia and New Jersey endorse such a route with or without the involvement of higher education. Georgia currently offers programs for prospective teachers in math, science, and foreign languages. School systems may furnish all or parts of the programs. Three options for preparation on the job are possible: (a) the internship and all course work taken through a school; (b) the internship offered through a school system's staff development program, with course work taken at a college or university in the evenings and on weekends; or (c) the internship and all course work available through a college or university (the internship nonetheless being done in a school).

Internships such as those in Georgia and New Jersey appear to be monitored more for assessment than for assistance. When assistance is the emphasis, it is different in nature and scope than it is for people who have had previous study in education or student teaching. The frame of reference is not that of helping an individual who has been prepared to teach get through a transition period of learning to apply and refine what has been learned; rather, it is one of working with beginners who must combine study and analysis at the same time that they try to survive at a full-time teaching job.

Impact at the State Level

Beginning teacher programs have spread mainly through policy initiatives at the state level. Thirteen states now require an internship or residency for the beginning teacher (Mastain, 1988). Nine other states are piloting programs. Georgia requires the internship for those who have not completed a teacher preparation program.

Of the 13 states represented in our sample, 8 provide some funding, either through grants for pilot programs or according to the number of teachers or students served. For example, according to Mastain (1988), Florida pays $1.70 per unweighted full-time-equivalent student; Indiana, $600.00 per support teacher;

North Carolina, $100.00 per beginning teacher. Some states not included in our sample pay support teachers more than $900.00 per year. Support for beginning teachers requires financial commitments. Implementation has been hampered in states that have mandated support programs, but provided no funds, such as Ohio.

Assistance Versus Assessment

Requiring completion of a probationary period for certification that includes demonstrating teaching competence brings assessment into contention with the concept of a support system. It raises the issue of the effectiveness of an assistance program delivered by support teachers (or a support team) that will also evaluate the beginner. Twelve of the 13 states with mandated assistance programs involve support teachers in assessment as well as assistance (Mastain, 1988).

Florida mandated its Beginning Teacher Program in 1982 to ensure that teachers who were awarded a professional teaching certificate had demonstrated the state's minimum essential generic competencies. In Broward County's version of the program, assistance and assessment are separated. The support team consists of a peer teacher, another professional educator, and a building-level administrator. The first two assist, the third assesses.

In Nash County, North Carolina's mentoring program, assistance and assessment are combined. Teachers who want to be support teachers must complete North Carolina's Effective Teacher and Performance Appraisal training before applying. The primary role of the support teacher as described by the state of North Carolina is twofold: (a) to assess the demonstrated performance of the novice teacher and (b) to facilitate the development and the refinement of essential practices and skills. In the mentoring program of Wake County, North Carolina, support teachers must engage in a two-semester sequence of training that includes performance appraisal.

The Teacher Induction Program in the Ohio County Schools of Wheeling, West Virginia, includes assistance only. West Virginia has not identified generic competencies that all beginning teachers must demonstrate.

The Arizona Teacher Residency Project uses an assessment instrument for a purpose different from assessment for certification—development of a teacher education data base. The project is designed to determine whether a teacher observation instrument can be used in an undergraduate program before and during student teaching and during the teaching internship to assess readiness for certification. Support teachers and beginning teachers in the residency program learn and practice the observation skills necessary to use the instrument. Assessment is formative to develop an instructional improvement plan.

Although many of the programs that were surveyed contain both assistance and assessment functions, the authors of this monograph [as well as the ATE's Commission on the Teacher Induction Process (Brooks, 1987)] hold that if an assistance program is to be effective, the role of the support teacher should be restricted to assistance and other personnel should be charged with assessment for employment or certification. Removing all barriers to the development of a trust relationship between the beginner and the support teacher is essential so that the novice can confide needs and weaknesses as well as strengths and talents.

One can easily discern that state legislatures have been the driving force behind the induction movement, which includes beginning teacher assistance programs. However, assessment has been a major goal in these state programs, assistance a secondary focus.

Summary

Although based on limited evidence, our survey indicates that programs to assist beginning teachers appear to have had a variety of demonstrated impacts on teachers, school systems, teacher education programs, and state-level activities. Several programs have documented retention of beginning teachers, improvement of their well-being, and enhancement of their teaching performance. Program leaders report testimony from support teachers of professional growth and satisfaction as well as increased knowledge about teaching and helping beginners. Programs can strengthen inservice professional development efforts, expand career-ladder opportunities, and encourage renewed consideration of the impact of context on success in teaching. In teacher education, beginning teacher assistance programs have contributed to more collaboration with public schools, greater scrutiny of generic competencies in teaching, and a larger amount of data gathered to assist in curriculum revision. State legislators, boards, and departments of education have initiated movement, provided financial assistance, and explored the issue of assessment versus assistance.

Other Possible Impacts

Having identified these actual impacts, we are reminded quickly of other possible areas of impact and the need to gather more information from existing programs. Several kinds of impact have not yet garnered much attention. Indirectly, mention has been made of the impact on teachers' salaries. Support teachers in some situations receive stipends for working with beginners, or they serve in that role only after moving up on a career ladder. Also, beginners in some intern programs receive less than a regular teacher's salary.

Impact on teacher work load has also been given scant attention. Time for support teachers to work with beginners has been provided in just a few systems. The gradual induction of the beginner into teaching ideally requires a lighter teaching load, but that adjustment is made in very few programs.

Impact on approaches to selecting and hiring teachers as yet has gone unnoticed or unreported. Some of the consequences of beginning teacher assistance programs should give clues to criteria that can be employed in recruiting novices.

The impact of beginning teacher assistance programs on the roles of teachers is inherent in much of what has been reported in this chapter. Inevitably programs to help beginners will, with other initiatives such as career ladders, cause an examination of teacher roles. The matter has at least two dimensions: whether all teachers should continue to serve in essentially the same role, as they do in most school districts; and whether a teacher's role should alter or expand with experience, so that the fruits of growth can be shared and so that teachers can aspire to new challenges as their careers proceed. Exploring teacher roles can also lead to exploring new staffing patterns, different team arrangements, and other structural changes in school organization—all possible outcomes of the assistance approaches being tried with new teachers.

A number of other kinds of impact need study: whether and how beginning teacher assistance programs influence student achievement and staff development; how state assessment requirements influence the creativity and the flexibility of beginning teachers; and how support programs affect innovation in teacher education.

Impact will, of course, never be adequately documented or appraised unless evaluation of programs is an integral part of every beginning teacher assistance program. The next chapter addresses this topic.

References

Blackburn, J. (1977). *The first-year teacher: Perceived needs, intervention strategies and results.* Paper presented at the annual meeting of the American Educational Research Association, New York. (ERIC Document Reproduction Service No. ED 135 768).

Brooks, D. M. (Ed.). (1987). *Teacher induction: A new beginning.* Reston, VA: Association of Teacher Educators. (ERIC Document Reproduction Service No. 279 607).

Franklin County–Ohio State University Induction Project. (1988). *The right stuff: Essential elements for structuring an induction program.* Columbus, OH: Ohio State University.

Henry, M. (1988, June). *Certification Renewal Experiences Designed to Improve Teaching: Report of a multiple support system for first-year teachers.* Paper presented at the Leadership Academy on Planning and Implementing Induction and

Beginning Teacher Support Programs, sponsored by the Association of Teacher Educators, National Academy for Leadership in Teacher Education, and Rhode Island College, Providence, RI.

Huling-Austin, L. (1988). *The influence of context on the teacher induction process.* Paper presented at the Leadership Academy on Planning and Implementing Induction and Beginning Teacher Support Programs, sponsored by the Association of Teacher Educators, National Academy for Leadership in Teacher Education, and Rhode Island College, Providence, RI.

Indiana Department of Education. (1988). *Beginning Teacher Internship Program handbook.* Indianapolis, IN: Author.

Marockie, H., & Marockie, M. (1988, June). *Teacher induction program: A three-year orientation and support system for beginning teachers.* Paper presented at the Leadership Academy on Planning and Implementing Induction and Beginning Teacher Support Programs, sponsored by the Association of Teacher Educators, National Academy for Leadership in Teacher Education, and Rhode Island College, Providence, RI.

Maryland State Department of Education, Staff Development Branch, and Research for Better Schools. (1987). *Perspectives on teacher induction: A review of the literature and promising program models.* Baltimore: Author.

Mastain, R. (Ed.). (1988). *Manual on certification and preparation of educational personnel in the United States.* Sacramento, CA: National Association of State Directors of Teacher Education and Certification.

Odell, S. J. (1988, June). *A model university–school system collaboration on teacher induction.* Paper presented at the Leadership Academy on Planning and Implementing Induction and Beginning Teacher Support Programs, sponsored by the Association of Teacher Educators, National Academy for Leadership in Teacher Education, and Rhode Island College, Providence, RI.

Schlechty, P., & Vance, V. (1983). Recruitment, selection and retention: The shape of the teaching force. *Elementary School Journal, 83,* 469–487.

Summers, J. A. (1987). *Summative evaluation report: Project CREDIT.* Terre Haute, IN: Indiana State University, School of Education.

Waters, L. B., & Watson, M. (1988, June). *Oakland–California State University Hayward New Teacher Support Project.* Paper presented at the Leadership Academy on Planning and Implementing Induction and Beginning Teacher Support Programs, sponsored by the Association of Teacher Educators, National Academy for Leadership in Teacher Education, and Rhode Island College, Providence, RI.

Wildman, T., & Magliaro, S. (1988, June). *Five years of research and program development in teacher induction.* Paper presented at the Leadership Academy on Planning and Implementing Induction and Beginning Teacher Support Programs, sponsored by the Association of Teacher Educators, National Academy for Leadership in Teacher Education, and Rhode Island College, Providence, RI.

-5

Evaluation of Beginning Teacher Assistance Programs

Richard S. Kay

Programs in education, especially new ones such as those to provide assistance to beginning teachers, are under increasing pressure from government, citizens group, and the profession itself to demonstrate their value. This requires careful monitoring and documentation, so that interested parties can be informed. The purpose of this chapter is to share ideas that educators may find useful in designing a systematic, comprehensive approach to evaluating beginning teacher assistance programs. Evaluation is a major function of program management and is presented in that context.

Evaluation as a Process

Evaluation is a process that should follow a set and a sequence of steps and procedures designed to provide information for informed decision making. Steps and procedures vary greatly, depending on the orientation of the evaluator and the purpose of an evaluation. The reader should review available alternatives, which are described in great detail in a number of highly respected evaluation texts. Some excellent source books include Cronbach (1982) and Worthen and Sanders (1987).

The following steps and procedures are illustrative of many evaluation models; they are not intended or recommended as a model in themselves.

1. Identify the purpose of the evaluation.
2. Identify the critical decisions to be made and the related questions to be answered before making each decision.

3. Identify the types of information needed to answer each question and the potential sources and methods for obtaining the information.
4. Design or develop appropriate instruments and procedures for collecting, analyzing, and reporting the information.
5. Collect, analyze, and summarize the information.
6. Report the information to program decision makers.
7. Make the decisions.
8. Implement the decisions.

These steps simplify a complex process. Each step includes several subtasks, all of which must be completed. For example, Step 4, design or develop appropriate instruments, involves operationalizing each variable to be assessed, writing specific instructions for the administration of the instrument, validating the instrument to ensure valid data collection, etc. An explication of these subtasks can be found in texts on evaluation.

Designing a Program Evaluation System

Program evaluation requires a planned structure through which it can be implemented and controlled. Ideally it is an integral part of the total program and a permanent part of the management system. As such, it is much less likely to be forgotten or to be implemented only on a crisis basis (this is so often the case in educational programming).

A prerequisite to designing a system for program evaluation is to plan the complete program, including the system for conducting the affairs of the program and delivering the program according to plan—that is, the management system. The definition of *manager* used in this chapter is broad, including anyone at any level of program operation who is involved in making decisions about program operation. Under this definition classroom teachers are often considered program managers. The components of management systems and the levels of management within the program are two critical areas to consider in program planning.

Management Systems

Program management is a process with three primary objectives: (a) to plan program outcomes and operation, (b) to oversee program operation and ensure that the planned outcomes are achieved effectively and efficiently, and (c) to evaluate program performance by analyzing the outcomes of program operation, determining the nature and the sources of difference between planned and achieved outcomes, and identifying needed corrective actions. Management systems typically include the following parts: goals and objectives; structure; assigned responsibilities; performance criteria and standards; operating principles, policies, and rules; information networks; and a mechanism for decision making and follow-up.

Goals and Objectives

Goals are broad statements of purpose, the focal point of program organization and operation. All aspects of a well-organized program are directed toward achieving its goals. Goals for programs to assist beginning teachers may include increasing their instructional effectiveness, providing them with support to reduce the trauma of starting a new career, and familiarizing them with the operation and the policies of their employing school districts.

Structure

Structure is the combination of resources and methods used to achieve goals. Programs may have similar goals, but employ widely different resources and methods to accomplish them. Resources may comprise personnel, finances, physical facilities, support groups, and materials; methods may encompass curriculum, training procedures, administrative theory, and incentive programs. The arrangement and the combination of resources and methods will be unique to each program and reflect its stated goals.

Assigned Responsibilities

Goals can be accomplished only when specific subtasks are successfully completed. These subtasks must be identified, and responsibility for the completion of them must be assigned to a manager or managers. Each responsibility should be accompanied by appropriate authority to manage the corresponding area of program operation and by a definition of the limits within which that authority can and ought to be exercised. Accomplishing a goal of increasing the instructional effectiveness of beginning teachers would require that instructional assistance be made available to new teachers according to their needs. Providing such assistance would be a responsibility assigned to a manager (probably a support teacher).

Performance Criteria and Standards

Performance criteria and standards describe the quality of performance necessary for successful program operation. They serve as a model for training personnel and as a checkpoint for determining the quality of program operation. Observed program operation can be compared with planned operation as specified in the performance criteria and standards. Examples of performance criteria and standards include the following:

1. The support teacher or group observes the beginning teacher at least once a week for a minimum of 30 minutes and afterward provides feedback, identifying specific areas of strength and weakness in teaching behavior.
2. The building administrator participates in postobservation feedback sessions with each beginning teacher at least once a month.

Other items might address the quality of the observations and the feedback. With such specifications the personnel in charge of observation know what is expected. Also, the manager has a point of comparison for determining if adequate support is being provided. Criteria and standards should be specified for each point at which success or failure in performance will affect the quality of program operation.

Operating Principles, Policies, and Rules

Operating principles are broadly defined guidelines for the decisions that must be made for efficient and effective program operation. Principles allow the manager to be flexible without losing sight of goals. An example of an operating principle is, "The responsibility for improving teaching behavior ultimately lies with the beginning teacher; the responsibility of all others is considered support." Policies and rules are more restrictive statements, formulated by line leaders to guide managers in making operational decisions that are congruent with the limits of their authority and with program goals. An operating rule may be, "The support teacher or group does not visit the classroom of the beginning teacher for observation without an invitation from him or her." The principles, policies, and rules will vary according to the goals of the particular beginning teacher assistance program.

Information Networks

The remaining two components of program management, information networks and a mechanism for decision making and follow-up, provide the framework for program evaluation. Effective management requires that valid information be collected and made available to managers in time for them to make prompt, informed decisions. Information networks are designed according to management decisions. For example, managers of beginning teacher assistance programs may want to know if the assistance being provided is in fact enhancing the instructional performance of beginning teachers in the classroom.

Three information networks seem most relevant for a beginning teacher assistance program: (a) one to assess the need and to define the parameters for providing what is found to be necessary or advisable, (b) one to determine if the program is operating as designed, and (c) one to determine if the program is meeting the need for which it was designed. Elaboration on these information networks is provided in a later section, Planning the Program.

Mechanism for Decision Making and Follow-Up

The information that managers obtain through the various networks should result in decisions designed to enhance program operation, and there should be a specific, planned mechanism to ensure their implementation. For example, managers monitoring the effectiveness of a seminar for beginning teachers may receive information indicating that the teachers consider the seminar a waste of their time and feel no better prepared to provide quality instruction after taking the seminar than they did before. The seminar is expensive in many ways and needs to be modified to produce the outcomes intended. Management decides to redesign the seminar to reflect the inputs from teachers. According to plan, the decision, along with the input from teachers, is communicated to those responsible for planning and teaching the seminar.

Management Levels

Most beginning teacher assistance programs will be managed at more than one level, the number depending on size and complexity. All levels of management must be included in the total program description. At the top will be Level 1, the group ultimately responsible for the total operation of the program. Level 1 management may be a certification board in the state department of education, a consortium of educational agencies, teacher training institutions, or a state office. Level 2 management is a category that includes all levels of management between Levels 1 and 3. Likely groups in this category are indicated in the illustration that follows. Level 3 management is the participant, the beginning teacher. The individual teacher is considered management because he or she usually has some decision-making opportunities and powers that will affect program operation to a degree.

Management levels are illustrated in the following description of a hypothetical beginning teacher assistance program. The structure is only one of numerous possibilities.

The state legislature passes a law requiring that all teachers new to any school district in the state participate in a beginning teacher assistance program. The responsibility for designing, implementing, and overseeing the program is delegated to the state department of education and is specifically assigned to the certification and staff development office. An advisory committee is formed with representatives from school districts, teacher education institutions, and teacher organizations. With input from the advisory committee, the certification and staff development office develops and implements a plan. It specifies that local programs are to be administered by individual school districts according to an organization they determine. District-level organizations must include representatives from the school district and the local teacher union. Teacher education institutions are to serve as resources.

Level 1 management in this statewide program is the certification and staff development office. The state legislature is not part of the management structure because it has reserved no powers to itself to administer the program, and the advisory committee is not part because it does not have decision-making power or responsibility. Level 2 management includes the organizations established within individual school districts. Some give individual schools management responsibilities; therefore they qualify as Level 2 management. Other districts administer their program at the district level, eliminating the individual school as a management level. Support teachers or groups within schools may be included as Level 2 management because they have decision-making authority. Beginning teachers in the program constitute Level 3.

Figure 1
Planning Matrix for a Hypothethical Beginning Teacher Assistance Program

Management Components	Levels of Management				
	Level 1	Level 2		Level 3	
	State	District	School	Support	Teacher
Goals and objectives	Decrease number of qualified teachers who elect to leave profession during first three years of teaching.	Familiarize beginning teachers with district operating policies and procedures.	Orient new teachers to content and time-table of prescribed district curriculum.	Facilitate interaction of new teachers with other faculty in building.	Establish effective program of discipline in classroom.
Structure					
Assigned responsibilities					
Performance criteria and standards					
Operating principles, policies, and rules					
Information networks					
Mechanism for decision making and follow-up					

Planning the Program

Program planning is not linear. Compressing a description of it into a few pages oversimplifies a complex process. This chapter is not intended to be a treatise on planning, but a presentation of some helpful techniques.

Addressing the seven components and each level of management in a systematic way will help planners develop a more comprehensive program plan. To illustrate, the hypothetical program described earlier is used.

First, the purpose of the program must be identified. At this initial stage of planning, the statement of purpose need not be refined.

Next, a basic management structure should be identified. This basic structure will undoubtedly be modified as planning continues. Using the seven components of management systems as the vertical dimension and the levels of management as the horizontal dimension, a planning matrix such as that which appears in Figure 1 can be created.

The hypothetical beginning teacher assistance program has five management levels: Level 1 is the certification and staff development office (state). Level 2 comprises three levels: individual school districts/teacher organizations (district), individual schools (school), and support faculty or groups within the schools (support). Level 3 is the beginning teachers (teacher). The planning matrix for this program is 5 x 7 and includes 35 cells. Each cell represents a portion of the total program and should be made explicit in writing.

Following are sample goals for each of the management levels. One goal for each level is included in Figure 1 to illustrate use of the matrix.

Goals at the State Level
1. To assist beginning teachers toward increased productivity and professional well-being in their first years of teaching.
2. To decrease the number of qualified teachers who elect to leave the profession during their first three years of teaching.

Goals at the District Level
1. To familiarize beginning teachers with district operating policies and procedures.
2. To orient beginning teachers to instructional and other services available through district funds, programs, and personnel.

Goals at the School Level
1. To orient beginning teachers to the timetable of the prescribed district curriculum.
2. To orient beginning teachers to building policies and procedures.
3. To welcome beginning teachers into the social structure of the building faculty.

Goals at the Support Level
1. To provide assistance to beginning teachers in handling the problems and the tasks of teaching.
2. To facilitate interaction between beginning teachers and other faculty and staff in the building.

Goals at the Teacher Level
1. To establish an effective program of discipline in the classroom.
2. To help the students learn the content specified for their grade level.
3. To establish a good working relationship with parents.

These goals should not be taken as a prescription for other programs. They only illustrate the different types of goals that may be set at the various levels of management. Goals may not be the same at all levels, but they should be consistent across levels.

The process of planning and specifying the program continues until the first five components—goals and objectives, structure, assigned responsibilities, performance criteria and standards, and operating principles, policies, and rules—are described at each management level. The remaining two components, information networks and mechanism for decision making and follow-up, are the basic elements of the evaluation system.

Information Networks

In the earlier discussion of information networks, three were identified as relevant for beginning teacher assistance programs, and each had a specific purpose: (a) to conduct a continuing needs assessment, (b) to monitor program operation, and (c) to determine program effectiveness. Each of the networks must be planned to complete the seven steps and procedures of the evaluation process, as outlined earlier.

Information Networks—Needs Assessment

Step 1 in the evaluation process is to identify the purpose of the evaluation. The main purpose of the needs assessment is to determine if there is a legitimate need for the product or the service.

Step 2 is to identify critical decisions that management must make and the related questions that must be answered first. (The list of decisions and questions that follows is not exhaustive.)

Decision 1

Is beginning teachers' need for help of sufficient magnitude in terms of the number of teachers or the severity of the need, to justify the investment of time and resources beyond those currently committed?

Questions to Be Answered
1. What proportion of beginning teachers report significant job-related difficulties during their first years of teaching?
2. What proportion of beginning teachers demonstrate significant job-related difficulties?
3. Do the reported and/or demonstrated problems of beginning teachers reflect a continuing or a temporary need?

Decision 2

Can a formal program provide the type of assistance most generally and urgently needed?

Questions to Be Answered
1. Are the areas of need and difficulty related to the existing curriculum of teacher preparation programs?
2. Is beginning teachers' need for assistance inherent in the circumstances surrounding the first year of teaching, or is it caused by a shortcoming in teacher preparation programs?

The quality of evaluation will be largely determined by the quality of the decisions and the depth of the questions identified. Superficial decisions and inadequate questions will not provide the insight that makes for good program decisions.

In Step 3, program planners identify the type of information needed to answer adequately the questions related to each decision. The information gathered will affect the quality of the answer to each question. In deciding what information is needed and where that information can be obtained, program planners should ensure that the information collected (a) addresses all aspects of the question, (b) is valid, (c) comes from reliable sources, and (d) can be cross-validated using other sources.

The first decision identified in the needs assessment is whether beginning teachers' need for assistance is of sufficient magnitude to warrant formal assistance. One of the questions to be answered in relation to this decision is, "What proportion of beginning teachers report significant job-related difficulties during their first years of teaching?" What type of information is needed to answer this question, and where can it be obtained?

The question calls for data on the significant difficulties that beginning teachers perceive. The data should focus on the proportion of beginning teachers reporting job-related problems that they feel are significant, the number of beginning teachers reporting the same problems, and the nature of the difficulty. This information must be obtained from teachers during their first years of teaching. If all beginning teachers cannot be surveyed, a representative sample should be drawn from a defined population. If the program is a state one, the population may be beginning teachers employed in the state, or it may be that group plus beginning teachers trained in the state and employed elsewhere.

Designing information-gathering instruments and information-handling procedures, and then collecting, analyzing, and reporting information are Steps 4, 5, and 6 of the evaluation process. Who will develop the instruments and the procedures? Who will handle the information at each step? (In most cases, developers and handlers are different personnel.) These are only a few of the questions that program planners will have to address.

The following guidelines may be helpful in designing information-collection, -analysis, and -reporting procedures:

1. Data-collection procedures should be as unobtrusive as possible. Interruptions should be kept to a minimum.
2. Information should be gathered in a form that minimizes costs related to collection, analysis, summary, and reporting.
3. Information should be summarized and reported in a form directly related to the question(s) to be answered.

The structure planned to accomplish Steps 1–6 should be described in writing following the same procedure suggested for other management components. Attention should be given to appropriate structure at each level of management. Step 4, for example, designing instruments and procedures, might be assigned to program personnel at the district level, whereas Step 5, collecting and analyzing data, may be assigned to personnel at the school level. A step may be assigned to more than one management level; if so, it should be described as such.

Steps 7 and 8 as related to the needs assessment should be described under the final management component, a mechanism for decision making and follow-up. Steps 1–6 are now applied to the two remaining information networks.

Information Networks—Program Operation
In regard to Step 1, the main purpose of the program operation network is to monitor all aspects of program operation to determine if the program is operating as intended. The program description details intended operation and provides a standard for assessing actual operation.

For Step 2, possible decisions and questions are as follows:

Decision 1

Are beginning teachers receiving assistance and feedback from support teachers that is specific to their unique needs?

Questions to Be Answered
1. Are beginning teachers being given the opportunity to express their individual needs and desires for assistance?
2. Are support teachers and groups experienced and expert in the areas of greatest need expressed by beginning teachers?

Decision 2

Are management responsibilities being completed at the level to which they are assigned?

Questions to Be Answered
1. Is assistance for beginning teachers being coordinated through support teachers or groups?
2. Are beginning teachers initiating requests for help through their assigned support teachers or groups?

The program-monitoring network has a vast range of applications; any segment or the total operation may be evaluated within its framework. The list of decisions and questions can be almost endless. Comments and suggestions made in the discussion of the needs assessment network can be repeated for the program-monitoring and program-effectiveness networks.

Information Networks—Program Effectiveness

In regard to Step 1, the purpose of this network is to determine whether the training and the experience provided are effective in preparing the participants for their job responsibilities.

In regard to Step 2, following are a couple of decisions that managers may need to make concerning program effectiveness:

Decision 1

Do the program activities adequately address all areas of need that are critical to improving the confidence and the productivity of beginning teachers?

Questions to Be Answered
1. Are there identifiable patterns of continued anxiety and/or weakness in the behavior of participants after they have had assistance during the first year(s)?
2. Do teachers who have had formal assistance perform any differently in the classroom than experienced teachers or beginning teachers who have not received assistance?

Decision 2
Are the benefits to programs in the schools where beginning teachers are employed sufficient to justify the expense of the assistance program?

Questions to Be Answered
1. What benefits to the school systems can be identified that result from the beginning teacher assistance programs?
2. What are the costs associated with assistance programs in money, human effort, and diversion of experienced teachers from working directly with students?

The reader may feel overwhelmed by the magnitude of the design task. Program designers need to understand the purposes and the operations of program evaluation systems, but unless they are experienced as evaluators, they would be well advised to seek help from professionals in designing their systems. It may seem easy to ask questions and collect data. Asking the right kind of question can make the difference between an insightful evaluation and a data-collection project. Evaluators can be very helpful to program managers in obtaining the right kind of information to assist in effective and efficient program operation. The type of evaluation advocated in this chapter is extensive and requires a commitment of time and money if it is to be done well. Once designed, a well-conceived evaluation system can also provide continuing research opportunities that should not be overlooked.

Summary

The purpose of this chapter is to share ideas on how to develop a comprehensive system for program evaluation as an integral and continuing part of a beginning teacher assistance program. Evaluation can be abridged into a seven-step process of information gathering and decision making. All processes, evaluation included, require an organization or a structure to carry them to completion. Seven components and three levels of management systems provide a structure that enables managers to plan, implement, and operate programs effectively.

In planning an evaluation system, the process of evaluation is combined with the components and the levels of management. Three information networks are appropriate for an evaluation system for beginning teacher assistance programs. These networks, each serving a specific purpose, combine to make a comprehensive system for information gathering and decision making. Related to each network are decisions that management must make and questions that management must answer before making the decisions. The questions are used to guide the identification and the selection of information to gather, handle, and make available to decision makers. The final touch on evaluation systems is provided when a mechanism for making and implementing decisions is planned and made explicit.

References

Cronbach, L. J. (1982). *Designing evaluations of educational and social programs*. San Francisco: Jossey-Bass.

Worthen, B. R., & Sanders, J. R. (1987). *Educational evaluation*. New York: Longman.

6

Starting a Beginning Teacher Assistance Program

Roy A. Edelfelt and Peggy Ishler

The preceding chapters were designed to whet appetites and spark interest in beginning teacher assistance programs. Whether anything happens, however, usually depends on local need and readiness. Often a big problem is how to get started. One person with conviction may introduce the idea, but successfully implementing a program requires widespread awareness and interest in the potential of assisting beginners. Lay policy makers and educators alike must recognize the benefits to the novice and to the school district.

Beginning teacher assistance programs are in a stage of development at which more is known about the right questions to ask than about the best prescriptions for starting a program. As a consequence, suggesting a course of action that will work in any state or school district is inappropriate. However, enough experience and evidence are available to indicate some of the questions that can guide people who want to initiate a program and that might be useful to those who have programs under way. Asking the right questions and finding answers to them in a specific context is a productive way to make progress.

Beginning teacher assistance programs require more than assigning skillful, experienced teachers to work with novices. They call for an awareness that beginners need help, some agreement about purposes, data on the problems of beginners, a hard look at what it takes to help beginners, a plan to structure a program and define participants' roles, and a host of other information on what and how assistance can be provided and by whom. Information on all those points is reported in Chapters 1–5.

In this chapter seven important considerations for putting together a beginning teacher assistance program are addressed: starting, seeking essential policy and support, building awareness, recognizing the importance of the school principal, examining the role of the college of education, understanding professional governance, and considering the process of educational change. The seven areas are explored with questions.

Starting

The information, the opinions, and the research data in this monograph tell about the ways in which selected beginning teacher assistance programs are functioning. An easy way to launch a program is to copy what others are doing, and at times that may be effective. Learning from the experience of others certainly is possible. However, in the best scenario a program fits the goals, the people, and the context of a particular situation. Before considering how a program can be devised to fit a local situation, it is usually wise to determine whether a program should be started.

Need and Prospects

Considering whether to embark on a program to assist beginning teachers requires raising questions about the need and the possibilities for such a program:

1. Is a program to assist beginning teachers needed?
   - How many new teachers does the system hire each year?
   - Will many new teachers be hired in the next few years?
   - Are beginning teachers expected to be largely self-sufficient?
   - Have new teachers left the system after one or two years? Why?
   - Do hiring procedures help ensure a fit between new teachers and the level, the subject, and the type of student to be taught?
   - Do beginning teachers in the school district need help? Why? What kind?

- Do new teachers have complaints or apparent problems?
- Are students shortchanged when a beginning teacher has difficulty during the first year or two of teaching?
- Has there been documentation of the difficulties that beginners face?

2. What are the purposes of a program to assist beginning teachers?
   - Are there belief statements that provide a basis for establishing an assistance program for beginning teachers?
   - Is the purpose primarily to assist beginning (new) teachers in making the transition from collegiate study to professional practice?
   - Is the purpose to orient a new teacher into the culture of a school or a school district?
   - Is the purpose to provide an induction into the teaching profession?
   - Is the purpose to make preservice preparation, induction, and career-long development a continuum?
   - Is the purpose related to efforts to *assess the adequacy* of new teachers?
   - If there is more than one purpose, is the relationship of purposes complementary?
   - Do the purposes reflect the district's general philosophy of education?

3. What should the goals of a program be?
   - Are the goals for the program to assist beginning teachers related to the purposes identified in *(2)*?
   - Can specific objectives be formed from the broad goals?
   - Should the objectives be stated in measurable terms?
   - Will the objectives be compatible with state requirements, district goals, and school needs?
   - Can the objectives help define the roles of all participants?

4. How will the program be initiated?
   - Has the program been mandated by the state or the school district? If so, how has the decree affected

attitudes toward beginning teachers and activities to assist them?

- Will the development of the program be a cooperative endeavor between the local school district, higher education institutions, teacher organizations, and the state department of education?
- How will the local program be influenced by state policy? Will forces outside the local district support the program, for example, with finances or technical assistance? Will outside forces constrain the local program with demands, such as regulations, paperwork, or a preconceived program design?
- Is the program seen as a part of the district's (and the state's) responsibility for professional development?
- Who should be involved in planning the program?
- Who should be responsible for maintaining and evaluating the program?

5. What factors might cause problems for beginners?
- What attitudes do experienced teachers and administrators in the school district have about beginning teachers?
- Are assignments for beginning teachers the same as those for veterans?
- Do beginning teachers receive the most difficult assignments and the heaviest loads?
- Are all beginners expected to succeed in any assignment?
- Does anyone take responsibility for discovering the problems of beginning teachers? Are objective data available on the experience of beginners?
- Is reassignment of beginners possible when severe problems occur?
- Do teachers and principals have a part in selecting new teachers?
- Do teachers and administrators see a need for a special effort to assist beginners?

6. What assistance do beginners need?

- How are the difficulties and the problems of beginning teachers ascertained?
- What kinds of problems do beginning teachers have locally?
- Are teachers encouraged to develop their own teaching styles?
- Can beginners become accepted by their faculty and still develop their own talents and skills as teachers?
- Should beginners be expected to solve their own teaching problems?
- Do novice teachers need an induction into the teaching profession?
- What kind of assistance do beginning teachers in the system need?
- What is the main focus in helping a beginner?
- Are beginners responsible for the difficulties they face?
- For how long should beginning teachers receive assistance?
- To what extent can a beginning teacher assistance program be planned, and to what extent must it be flexible so that it can respond to the needs of specific teachers?
- How much is known about beginning teacher assistance programs?

7. Who should assist the beginner?
- Can any good teacher or administrator serve as a support teacher for a beginning teacher?
- Should an assistance program for beginners be related to student teaching? To what extent are the two efforts alike?
- Are special skills and knowledge needed to help an adult learn?
- What criteria should be used in selecting support teachers?
- Who should be in charge of selecting support teachers?
- Do support teachers need special training? If so, what kind and how much?

- Who should or can train support teachers?
- How should the system assist support teachers?

8. What are the costs and the benefits of a beginning teacher assistance program?
   - Should beginners have a lighter teaching load than veterans?
   - Should support teachers be rewarded beyond their regular salary?
   - What benefits (other than money) should veteran teachers receive from a beginning teacher assistance program?
   - What relationship does a program for beginning teachers have to a career-ladder program?
   - What training do support teachers need? What will it cost?
   - What will a program to assist beginning teachers cost?
   - What are the benefits of a beginning teacher assistance program to beginners? . . . to support teachers? . . . to a school faculty? . . . to the school district?

9. What professional development activities should be part of every beginning teacher's experience?
   - Should the beginner be introduced to the community and the background of the students? How?
   - How should the beginner become familiar with the state's and the school district's courses of study, competency-testing requirements, and scope and sequence of the curriculum in his or her subject?
   - How should the beginner be introduced to the facilities of the school district?
   - How will the beginner become knowledgeable about the district's philosophy and procedures for evaluation?
   - Should activities be planned to meet the beginner's emotional needs and concerns as well as his or her professional needs?
   - Should beginners have opportunities to plan some of their own developmental experiences? What might some of those experiences be?

There are a variety of ways to probe these questions. Certainly they must be discussed by policy makers and leaders of a school district. Increasingly there is evidence that the involvement of both teachers and administrators is important to the success of changes in schools. In many schools there is also a readiness among teachers and administrators for more involvement by teachers.

If there is a disposition to involve teachers and administrators (and lay people), one way to use the preceding questions is to assemble the entire group (or a representative one) for discussion. One purpose of such a discussion is to obtain input from the people who will be most affected by the innovation. The nine questions should be available to all participants, but for discussion it will probably be more productive to divide participants into groups and assign a different question to each group. Groups of five to seven people are preferable. That size allows discussion time for everyone, provides an opportunity for group members to become acquainted, and includes enough people to stimulate the creation of ideas. If there are more than 63 people overall, two groups can discuss the same topic. Discussions are usually more successful when participants are interested in their topic, so they should be free to choose among the possibilities.

Each group should be asked to perform four tasks: (a) answer as many of the questions posed under its topic as possible, (b) add questions that come up that have not been included (and try to answer them), (c) indicate the additional information that it needs to respond to the questions it cannot answer, and (d) report the essence of its discussion and attitudes about the idea to the total group and to school authorities.

After groups report on these tasks, one of several alternatives may be evident. For example, there may be sufficient interest and information to warrant moving ahead with the idea; there may be no interest or need, in which case people can depart knowing that they have explored the possibility; or there may be interest, but a great need for more information. The latter is probably the most frequent outcome.

Seeking Essential Policy and Support

If the decision is to obtain more information, another area to probe is existing policy. Teachers and administrators usually have a host of questions about policy and budget, especially when a new program is proposed. Practitioners make many assumptions about such matters, but they are often very unclear about actual rules, regulations, financial considerations, and policies.

Most policies and budget decisions are made by the state legislature, the state board of education, the state department of education, and the local board of education. The degree to which implementation of any program is possible is usually determined by the adequacy of policy and budget.

Policy on assistance to beginning teachers is most likely to be addressed under the category of professional development. To entertain seriously the prospects for assisting beginners, teachers and administrators should know what license they have (or can obtain) to plan, staff, carry out, and evaluate a program. Policy is the rubric under which programs are sanctioned; budget allocations provide the funds to implement policy. Questions about policy and support will not be the same in every situation. To initiate their inquiry, teachers and administrators might ask whether there are policies and support in relation to the following:

1. The professional development of teachers, more specifically, assistance to beginning teachers
2. A budget allocation for professional development
3. Collaboration with local colleges and universities
4. Definitions of teachers' roles and functions
5. Standards and practices for cooperating teachers, helping teachers, or support teachers
6. A hierarchy of professional roles, responsibilities, and rewards.

These areas are illustrative; a local group can add to or delete from the list. Most important is that personnel raise questions relevant to their circumstances.

Initially there will probably be considerable ignorance and disagreement about existing policies. A frequent outcome for a group of educators discussing policy is to find that a great number of school practices are not set in policy or regulation. Practices relating to professional development are no exception. Consequently it is usually important in embarking on a beginning teacher assistance program to gain the kind of sanction from governing bodies that guarantees a good measure of support for the idea, sets up the parameters for a process, and encourages communication among appropriate individuals, groups, and policy makers.

Reactions and recommendations resulting from a discussion of the preceding issues should be reported to the board of education and the superintendent. If their response suggests moving ahead, next steps might be to start developing awareness of the problems and the tasks of the various participants in a beginning teacher assistance program.

Building Awareness

For a beginning teacher assistance program to function well, all of the people in the district who will be involved in the program should become sensitive to the importance of building a supportive environment.

Fostering Sensitivity to Being Helped and Helping

To create more sensitivity, one task is to develop greater awareness throughout the district of the need to help adult professionals get started. Sensitivity can be enhanced by having adults analyze how they have felt in the roles of being helped and helping. Most people have experienced both roles, often informally. Sharing recollections of such experiences can develop sensitivity to beginners and can help teachers and administrators explore how they can become better helpers.

With a little assistance from a person skilled in leading discussion groups, a school faculty or a representative group from several schools can be organized into discussion groups to talk about and report on the questions listed in Discussion Guide 1. Again, discussion may be most productive if participants are divided into small groups. Each small group should be given suggestions or directions for selecting a chair and a recorder. Also, each small group should be provided with butcher paper and a felt pen to record the responses and the personal vignettes that members of the small group agree should be reported back to the total group. Other help with procedures should be determined by leaders on the basis of an assessment of the skills and the sophistication of the participants. Someone should be charged with developing a summary of small group reports. Such a report

---

Discussion Guide 2

Conceptualizing the Role of the Helper

- Have you ever helped someone else improve his or her teaching?
- Was the helping relationship largely one-way, or was it mutual?
- Have you ever helped another teacher learn more about content, methods, or materials of teaching?
- How did your relationship with the teacher you helped develop? How did you become the one who helped another teacher learn?
- How did you know that you had become the one who helped another teacher learn?
- What did you do to help? What roles did you take that made you a teacher who helped another teacher learn? Were you a listener? . . . a mirror? . . . a counselor? . . . a resource person? . . . an adviser?
- Did you provide feedback, ask questions, give advice, coach, etc.?
- What role was most effective in your interaction with the teacher whom you helped?
- How much of your behavior was casual? . . . formal? . . . part of your recognized responsibility? . . . deliberate?

---

can be helpful in subsequent meetings on planning, training, and evaluation.

Next, questions such as those in Discussion Guide 2 will bring focus to assistance. These questions probe being a helper to others, more specifically, being a highly qualified, experienced teacher—a support teacher—who helps a beginner. Administrators can take part in discussing these questions too; they have all been teachers at some time and are constantly in the position of being helpers.

Most participants will be able to recall experiences of an informal nature. In these discussions as in the earlier ones, anecdotes should be collected because they are very graphic. For the discussion of these questions, the same small groups that were recommended for earlier questions can be reassembled, or participants can be regrouped to meet with different people. At the conclusion of the discussion, the deliberations of each group should be reported to the entire assemblage, and a summary record developed and stored for future use. Responses from the discussion of sensitivity can be helpful in planning support teachers' responsibilities and training.

No Best Place for All to Begin

The preceding ideas for places to begin will fit some situations. In many instances the suggested approaches and questions may not be quite the right tack, so adaptations will have to be made. Local interest and circumstances will provide cues as to the most appropriate point of departure. Many or most of the relevant questions have been raised, however. The order in which they are addressed is not important; what is important is that the exploration be comprehensive. Between the questions raised in this chapter and those asked or implied in the foregoing chapters, any school or school district will either invite or discover the issues that need to be addressed to get started.

In a dynamic system, however, the areas to probe seem never to end. There is always something new to discover. That makes educational improvement stimulating and exciting, but also a bit frustrating.

Further Questions

The remainder of this chapter raises further questions. Some of these questions involve the role of the school principal, the role of the college of education, and the way in which the assistance program will be governed. These areas may need attention early in the process of getting started because of their critical importance.

Recognizing the Importance of the Principal

The principal is particularly important because of the need for his or her participation and support. Much of the way in which a principal responds may be influenced by what the school district expects of the building leader. Questions that can bring out the importance of the principal are as follows:

- To what extent is the principal informed and concerned about the plight of beginning teachers?
- Does he or she recognize the needs of beginning teachers?
- Does he or she have training in supervision?
- Is he or she involved in selecting beginning teachers?
- Does the principal determine the assignments given beginning teachers?
- Does the school district expect principals to take major responsibility for the improvement of instruction?
- How much time does the principal have for observation and supervision?
- Does the principal have the latitude to provide released time for beginning and support teachers?
- Does the principal have sufficient control of the school budget to provide support for the beginning teacher?
- Does the principal work with institutions of higher education on other aspects of teacher education?
- Does the principal work with institutions of higher education in supporting student teachers in the school?
- Does the principal provide feedback to institutions of higher education on the performance of their graduates?

Examining the Role of the College

As is already apparent, preservice teacher education is closely related to inservice professional development. Being helped as a beginner is an extension of collegiate study. The first year is a test of the work of college professors, and it is the beginning of the new teacher's continuing education. College faculty want to know how well their programs have prepared beginners; they are becoming more interested in helping with the transition from study to practice and more concerned about providing greater assurance that beginners are ready to start teaching. Assisting their products in the beginning year(s) enables teacher educators to reexamine what they do in preservice programs and to make changes to better prepare their students for the real world of teaching. As a consequence, many schools of education are becoming partners with public schools in assisting beginners in the induction years. Such a prospect leads to another set of questions:

- Do colleges of education systematically follow up on their graduates in the first few years of teaching?
- Do they promote a continuous focus on the relationship between theory and practice in their professional education courses?
- Do they maintain a working relationship with public schools?
- Are professors from colleges of education and other higher education units working in the schools with teachers and administrators?
- Do the top administrators in colleges and universities see working with public schools as an integral part of teacher education?
- Do colleges of education consider working with public schools an important priority?
- Does the reward system in colleges and universities encourage professors to work with schools?
- Are there college and school personnel with joint appointments on college and school district faculties?
- Do colleges of education provide training and assistance to support teachers?
- Do colleges of education foster or undertake research and evaluation of beginning teacher assistance programs?

Understanding Professional Governance

The involvement of colleges in beginning teacher assistance programs broadens the scope of decision making and increases the need for attention to policy that provides for governance. Governance in the teaching profession includes the mechanisms that exist to regulate teacher preparation and practice. Professional governance is well established in the senior professions; in teaching, it is in its infancy. A variety of boards and commissions in the states are involved in governance. Their authority and responsibility vary. Beginning teacher assistance programs are relatively new; few commissions or boards have established standards for them. As a result, there is an opportunity to influence the content of the standards and the procedures for such programs.

In implementing a local beginning teacher assistance program, it is necessary to know existing policies and available support at the state level. Operating within and through state regulations requires deftness and political sophistication. Maneuvers certainly cannot be carried out successfully without an understanding of how teacher education is governed. Discussion of the following questions will help uncover essential information:

- How is teacher education and professional practice regulated in the state? By what officials or agencies?
- How and by whom are the functions of setting and monitoring standards and practice performed?
- Is there an established group on which school and college personnel are represented that oversees (governs) the functioning of teacher education?
- To whom is this governance group responsible? To whom does it report? How is its responsibility exercised? How is the group monitored?
- Does the governance group have a budget and personnel to ensure adequate and responsible operation?
- Does the regulation of teacher education and practice provide for an induction, orientation, or probationary period for beginning teachers?

- Does the state agency recognize induction as a phase of teacher education?
- Are there state policies and a state program to *assist* beginning teachers?
- Are there state policies and a state program to *assess* beginning teachers during the probationary years for certification purposes? If so, how are the assistance and assessment programs orchestrated?
- Are there principles on which the beginning teacher assistance program operates? If so, how were they established?
- Which institutions and agencies contribute to the budget of the beginning teacher assistance program?
- Is there a mechanism for identifying problems or potential difficulties in the beginning teacher assistance program?
- Is there a relationship between the governance of the beginning teacher assistance program and the governance of student teaching (and other field experiences)?
- Is attention to the beginning teacher considered a part of the professional development of teachers?

Considering the Process of Educational Change

A beginning teacher assistance program is inevitably part of the larger school system operation. The process of planning such a program and making it operational will influence the entire school system, in both major and minor ways. It is therefore important to consider the way in which a beginning teacher assistance program is started and, as far as possible, to employ the best of what is known about educational change.

When there is both an interest and a desire to begin a program to assist beginning teachers, it should as far as possible be designed to fit the schools in which it will operate. If the relevant decisions are made by the people who will function in that context, the program can be tailor-made to the locale, understood by those who will operate it, and owned by those whom it will affect. In the process of planning and initiating such a program, participants can create a plan in which they believe, and develop a commitment to it. Moreover, if progress is not satisfactory, participants can usually make the necessary changes.

Assumptions about the importance of involving people in planning and operating their own program have a basis in both research and experience. Such assumptions should operate in concert with other propositions about the process of change in education. The following questions and propositions are particularly relevant to instituting a beginning teacher assistance program:

- Is the district willing to commit itself to the program for three to five years? Change is a slow process. An innovation such as a beginning teacher assistance program must be sustained over a reasonable period before its impact can be fairly assessed.
- Are teachers, administrators, and board members involved in planning? For an innovation to make a difference, a critical mass of people should participate to ensure that the change will be absorbed into the social system of the school. All personnel affected should take part in ways appropriate to their roles. This means including administrators, teachers, and school board members in the planning, and involving beginning teachers in the evaluation after the program has been implemented.
- Have collaborative approaches been explored? Improvement is most apt to occur through cooperative action. Although many programs are mandated, opportunities for collaborative and cooperative approaches usually exist within designated guidelines.
- Have personnel been prepared in the change process? Teachers and other educators need knowledge about and skills in the change process. A beginning teacher assistance program requires more than additional information about the problems of novice teachers.
- Have model programs been examined? Access to the best and latest information on assistance programs and related efforts is essential.
- Does the program involve training for all involved? New or changed roles and functions (particularly for support

teachers and building-level administrators) require training. Incentives, rewards, and a strong, stable system of nurturance and assistance are particularly important for personnel who are trying innovative ideas and pioneering roles. There must be latitude to make mistakes, and encouragement to learn from them.

- Have the possible areas of impact been considered? Educators involved in innovations such as beginning teacher assistance programs must recognize the possible impact that such changes may have on the larger context in which they occur. For example, a school may change its placement and teaching load policies for beginners, its approaches to staff development, or the way in which teachers help one another.
- What financial support has been provided? Change and improvement usually cost money. A successful beginning teacher assistance program needs financial support. However, a school or a district initiating one will probably reap dividends that outweigh costs.
- Will evaluation procedures examine impact on students? The central purpose of schooling—student learning— should constantly be a basic goal of any innovation or change, including beginning teacher assistance programs. Teachers and administrators should carefully examine how assistance programs benefit instruction and hence student learning.

The questions and the procedures in this chapter are posed with the suggestion that the above notions about educational change form a reasonable basis on which to operate and that a cooperative process is the most productive approach. Cooperative decision making, which is inherent in current recommendations to empower teachers, is further enhanced when decisions are made close to the scene of action. For that reason, discussion of the foregoing questions will result in the most fruitful answers and actions if all the personnel (or a representative group of them) in schools considering a beginning teacher assistance program are involved. Lay people might also be included in appropriate ways.

Further, it can be advantageous to seek technical assistance from higher education faculty, state department of education staff, or other people with relevant experience and knowledge.

Conclusion

The intellectual process with which teachers are so well acquainted is a continuous one of questioning, experimenting, and discovering. The same process is applicable to developing and refining a beginning teacher assistance program. This chapter has raised some questions that address a number of the essential issues on the topic. Referring again and again to the preceding chapters and to other writings on beginning teachers as a program proceeds will add to one's knowledge base. The primary source of information and insight will probably be local experience, particularly if it is based on the kind of thorough evaluation outlined in Chapter 5.

Descriptions of Selected Beginning Teacher Assistance Programs

Descriptions included in this appendix were prepared from materials provided by project personnel who made presentations at the Leadership Academy on Planning and Implementing Induction and Beginning Teacher Support Programs, sponsored by the ATE's National Academy for Leadership in Teacher Education and Rhode Island College, in Providence, Rhode Island, June 10–12, 1988. The programs that are described were in operation as of those dates. Most remain operative as characterized—often with improvements instituted from further experience. In many cases, material has been paraphrased or copied directly from project documents without using quotation marks. Descriptions have not been checked with project personnel, so on occasion there may be inaccuracies. Descriptions may also suffer from being incomplete. Names and addresses of program directors are included for reference.

All programs give attention to the beginning teacher. Sometimes *beginning teacher* means anyone new to the district or the state. Many programs include both assistance and assessment. No attempt has been made to isolate programs in which the beginner is a person new to teaching or to single out programs devoted exclusively to assistance, even though the focus in this monograph is primarily assistance to the beginning teacher in his or her first year(s).

Programs are arranged alphabetically by state, then by name. Participating organizations are noted.

Arizona

Teacher Residency Project

Arizona State University, Northern Arizona University, and the Center for Educational Development in collaboration with 60 school districts

The Arizona Teacher Residency Project (ATRP) grew out of (a) an evaluation of undergraduate teacher education and (b) a study to examine the appropriateness of the ATRP instrument as a guide to the content of the undergraduate curriculum and the skill development of undergraduates. The desired outcome of the study was to tie preservice and inservice education together in a way that would enhance collaborative relationships between universities and public schools.

The Teacher Residency Project encompasses Arizona State (ASU), Northern Arizona University (NAU), the Center for Educational Development (CED) in Tucson, and 60 school districts throughout the state. It is funded by the state department of education. The common goal is to promote excellence in education by bringing the art and the science of teaching to the conscious level.

The Pima County Teacher Residency Program (CED) provides a 16-hour training program for mentor and resident teachers (teachers in their first, second, or third year). Mentors learn and practice the skills of observation, scripting, and analysis of teaching. They are also taught coaching and conferencing techniques and ways of working with resident teachers to develop instructional improvement plans.

The NAU program incorporates residency training as part of the teacher preparation program. It uses the ATRP instrument as the main source of data to document skill development of preservice teachers in student teaching. NAU provides residency training for cooperating teachers.

The Maricopa County Teacher Residency Project (ASU) also provides teacher residency training to mentors and resident teachers and is beginning to train the cooperating teachers who work with student teachers. The ASU/Maricopa Project is the research center for all three projects to evaluate training and the mentoring process, to provide feedback to teacher training institutions, and to assist participating school districts in identifying specific staff development needs.

For more information, contact Billie Enz or Gary Anderson at Arizona State University, Tempe, AZ 85287-1111; Cynthia Nelson at Northern Arizona University, Flagstaff, AZ 86011; and Don Lawhead or Barbara Weber at the Center for Educational Development, Tucson, AZ 85726.

California

Induction for the Beginning Teacher (IBT)

California State University at Chico in collaboration with 13 counties

The approach at California State University at Chico is to support beginning teachers in their struggle to make the transition from the college environment to the realities of teaching, and to provide skill development to help them become effective teachers who remain in the profession. The program has three major components: orientation, seminars, and follow-up. Particularly unique to the program is the use of monthly, learner-determined, interactive seminars using "terrestrial microwave," known as Instructional Television for Students (ITFS). The video component is one-way, but there is two-way audio interaction with experts. The use of ITFS provides an opportunity for all beginners to work with experts on professional development—a benefit these rural and isolated teachers are seldom afforded.

Before the school year begins, novice teachers receive three days of intensive orientation within their seminar group. Orientation includes familiarizing beginners with IBT, establishing a mood of positive support, and presenting the topics of several subsequent seminars to establish the program pattern and to provide opportunities for planning by teaching teams.

Each beginning teacher is a part of a teaching team, which includes the beginner and a trained *peer coach* (an experienced teacher of the same grade level and content area). The peer coach's responsibility is to support one or two beginners.

Teams are brought together monthly as a seminar group (in one location in each county) under the leadership of an experienced teacher who is trained to facilitate the seminars. Seminars focus on transferring the pedagogical understandings learned in college to teaching practice; helping formulate questions that will aid beginners in analyzing teaching situations and determining possible actions; suggesting skills and materials; and offering criteria by which beginners might select the most suitable and feasible skills and materials. Topics include classroom management and time management, professional relationships and responsibilities, student evaluation, motivation and methods, alternative lesson designs, self-evaluation, and more.

Following each seminar, teaching teams formulate action plans on seminar topics that fit the needs of individual beginning teachers. Between seminars, peer coaches observe, directly and through videotape, and provide feedback, support, and help that furnishes follow-up and reinforcement of concepts discussed in seminars. Assessments of individual teachers' performance are held in the strictest confidence and remain with the beginning teacher.

Seminar facilitators and peer coaches are given one week of intensive training in peer coaching; teacher observation; the development, the socialization, and the needs of beginning teachers; group process; and IBT expectations and responsibilities. Follow-up training is provided once a month during the year by instructional television and in two days on campus in the middle of the year.

For more information, contact Victoria L Bernhardt, director, Induction for the Beginning Teacher Program, College of Education, California State University, Chico, CA 95929-0224, 916/895-6165.

New Teacher Support Project
Oakland School District and California State University at Hayward

The New Teacher Support Project has been available to 25 beginning teachers from inner-city schools in Oakland since fall 1986. The program has three major goals: to increase the retention of new inner-city teachers; to increase the effectiveness of new inner-city teachers; and to develop a professional orientation among new inner-city teachers, particularly a commitment to continuing professional development.

The project's thesis is that new inner-city teachers need to learn that others have overcome the very real difficulties of urban teaching and have found it a rewarding career. The project seeks to combat the isolation of the novice and provide pragmatic support in addressing crises as they occur. This is done through the use of (a) the new teacher–mentor bridge and (b) teacher consultants. Through the bridge approach, beginners are provided with a mentor, an immediate personal contact and source of information as they face their first few weeks on the job. Teacher consultants, who are more carefully matched to beginners than mentors are, are trained to provide continuing assistance throughout the induction year. Both consultants and mentors are available for on-the-spot advice based on their own experience in similar schools. A more formalized vehicle for improving teaching skills is a biweekly release day, which allows new teachers to observe and be observed by their teacher consultant.

Further support is available through consultation with university consultants and university-based academic resource consultants, and sharing with fellow new teachers. University consultants provide general support and guidance and, being from outside the district, often provide a less threatening source of guidance than district personnel. They also bring a wider perspective on beginning teaching. Academic resource consultants help beginners enrich content with new ideas and materials. At the secondary level they individualize consultations, share university films and equipment, and frequently make classroom visits. For elementary school teachers, faculty teams provide workshops and consult with individuals, particularly to assist in math and science instruction. Informal sharing among beginners began serendipitously, but has now been formally incorporated into the biweekly project seminars.

Biweekly project seminars focus on effective teaching in inner-city schools. They provide an opportunity for carefully structured introduction and practice of new instructional methodologies, classroom management techniques, and cross-cultural education strategies. Techniques practiced in the seminar can be tried out during the week in the classroom and discussed in the informal seminar work group that meets during the week between seminars.

A broad overall purpose of the project is to develop professionalism in new teachers, which means helping them take on the attitudes of professionals. The project puts particular emphasis on two such attitudes: a sense of professional discretion or empowerment and an orientation to continuing professional development. In a variety of ways already mentioned—seminar work groups; relationships with teacher consultants, mentors, university consultants, and their peers; etc.—beginning teachers are encouraged to look to their colleagues for support and guidance and to develop their own resource network. The project also seeks to empower participants by treating them as professionals and allowing them professional discretion. Examples are the wide discretion that new teachers have (with their teacher consultants) in using a $700 Professional Resource Fund allotted to each of them, in designing their release days, and in determining the focus of university consultants' observations/feedback sessions.

The project emphasizes that professional development does not end with successful completion of the first year or the receipt of a credential. In a formal way this idea is incorporated in the Second-Year Follow-up component of the project: Second-year teachers receive four release days and four seminar sessions scattered throughout the year. In less formal ways project personnel try to set a tone, to instill the expectation of continuing professional development.

For more information, contact Cynthia Harris, project director, Office of Staff Development, Oakland Unified School District, 1025 Second Avenue, Oakland, CA 94606, or Louise Bay Waters, project director, Department of Teacher Education, California State University at Hayward, Hayward, CA 94542, 415/881-3072.

District of Columbia

Intern-Mentor Program

District of Columbia Public Schools

The goal of the Intern-Mentor Program is to promote the professional growth and development of beginning teachers, called interns, by having experienced teachers, called mentors, provide them with intensive assistance and guidance. The program is an on-the-job practicum in which the mentors, who still have roots in the classroom, share the realities of the classroom with interns. Mentors typically are chosen for two years and devote full-time to assisting no more than 10 interns. They spent substantial time with each intern, observing him or her at least once every two weeks and consulting more frequently on planning, teaching techniques, selection of materials, assessment of students, and classroom management. Mentors coach and train interns and finally evaluate their classroom performance.

The internship is the first year of a two-year probationary period that must be successfully completed before tenure can be granted. Year one begins before the opening of school with an orientation. Principals introduce interns to school policies and procedures, and mentors assist interns in planning, selection of appropriate materials, teaching strategies, and classroom management.

Throughout the year mentors provide classroom assistance to interns in the delivery of their instructional programs, help interns acquire materials and other resources, participate in supervising interns, encourage interns in professional development, and participate in evaluating interns. Intern activities are directed at problems generally faced by teachers at the beginning of their careers. However, to ensure program effectiveness, professional development also attends to subjects of need and interest to interns, which have often been such matters as communication skills, instructional technology, and academic learning time.

During the second year the intern who has successfully completed the first year receives concentrated support from the building principal and the appropriate department chairperson, periodic support from the first-year mentor. The intern who is identified as needing continued intensive support from a mentor teacher repeats relevant components of the first-year internship. The intern is evaluated by both the mentor teacher and the building principal, and their recommendations are forwarded to review officers for decision on renewal of the intern's contract for the second year. The program, then, not only offers professional development to the new teacher but screens out those who show little aptitude for the classroom.

Mentors are selected from applicants by a committee composed of teachers and administrators. Criteria for selection include such qualities as evidence of outstanding teaching ability, the recommendation of supervisors and peers, subject-matter expertise, commitment to teaching, willingness to assume challenging assignments, and ability to work with others. Upon completion of a two-year term, the mentor returns to his or her original assignment.

For more information, contact Joan W. Brown, director, Incentive Programs for Teachers, District of Columbia Public Schools, 415 12th Street, N.W., Room 805, Washington, DC 20004, 202/727-6251 and 727-6335.

Florida

Beginning Teacher Program
Florida Department of Education

The Florida program includes all new teachers, whether they are beginners or veterans and whether they were prepared in the state or in other locations. The program has been established and funded by the state legislature, which requires that each school district develop a plan to implement the program. The intent is that (a) new teachers document successful demonstration of minimum essential competencies (as established by the state) required in the state's criteria for approved teacher education programs and (b) support services be provided to the beginning teacher during the first year of employment in Florida.

Each beginning teacher is assigned a support staff of at least three members: a building administrator, a peer teacher, and another professional educator. Support staff conduct at least five observations, including one diagnostic, three formative, and one summative. The Florida Performance Measurement Program instrument is used in the evaluation process. School districts receive $1.70 per unweighted full-time-equivalent student to support the program. Inservice education for the beginning teacher and the support staff is provided through state-funded teacher education centers in all 67 school districts.

For more information, contact Patricia Cheaver, Bureau of Teacher Education, B-34, Department of Education, Collins Building, Tallahassee, FL 32399, 904/488-0642.

Beginning Teacher Program
Broward County

In Broward County, Florida, teachers beginning their first year are supported by a school-based team consisting of a peer teacher, another professional educator, and a building-level administrator. The beginner must attend a six-hour workshop held during the school day and prepare (with support team assistance) a professional development plan. The district's Beginning Teacher Program (BTP) provides funds for a substitute if one is required.

Peer teachers are experienced teachers who hold regular certificates and teach the same level and subject or service area as the beginner. The responsibilities of peer teachers include scheduling and completing at least two formative observations, coordinating substitute teachers and observation dates, assisting the beginning teacher in meeting the recommendations in the professional development plan, successfully completing BTP inservice training activities for support team members, and monitoring and signing off on progress indicated on the timeline checklist.

The other professional educator is a professionally trained and experienced educator—a teacher, a teacher education center director, a staff development specialist, a curriculum director, an instructional supervisor or specialist, or a college or university teacher educator. The other professional educator takes responsibility for scheduling and completing one formative observation, initiating contact with additional professional resources, attending support team meetings, assisting the beginning teacher in meeting the recommendations in the professional development plan, and successfully completing BTP inservice training for support team members. Both the peer teacher and the other professional educator are required to attend 10 hours of training after school hours.

The building-level administrator is a certified school-based administrator who is responsible for the evaluation of the beginning teacher. His or her role includes providing a school-based orientation, conducting a minimum of two screening/summative evaluations, checking off competencies, supervising the construction of the professional development plan, successfully completing BTP training activities for administrators, successfully completing Florida Performance Measurement System training in order to be an approved observer on the screening/summative observation instrument, and ensuring that timelines are met according to the checklist for the BTP.

The school-based principal is responsible for selecting the support team members; completing the final assessment form, which indicates whether or not the beginning teacher has successfully completed the program; signing and approving the competency demonstration checklist and the portfolio; successfully completing BTP inservice training activities for administrators; and successfully completing Florida Performance Measurement System training in order to be an approved observer.

Broward County also operates an alternative certification program for secondary school teachers with a bachelor's degree in an arts and science discipline who are teaching in that discipline. These teachers also participate in a year-long beginning teacher program and attend specifically designed courses at Florida Atlantic University. The course work is based on the Florida Performance Measurement System.

For more information, contact Carrie Sedinger, coordinator, Broward County Public Schools, Broward County, FL 33310, 305/765-6000.

Georgia

Alternative Certification Program for Critical Teaching Fields

Georgia Department of Education

The Georgia beginning teacher program is an alternative route to certification for secondary school teachers in science, mathematics, and foreign languages. It exists to alleviate a critical shortage in the state for teachers in these fields. The program, a one-year supervised classroom internship in the appropriate field, is open to holders of a bachelor's degree from regionally accredited colleges and universities in the three critical fields. It is organized in four major blocks (preplanning, fall quarter, winter quarter, and spring quarter) guided and evaluated by a support team. It also requires satisfactory completion of five staff development units. Suggested are courses in the special learning needs of children, curriculum, teaching methodology, and human growth and development.

Interns are assisted by a support team, which includes a mentor teacher, the school principal, and the local staff development specialist. Where available, a curriculum specialist is strongly recommended to be part of the team.

The mentor must be a skilled practitioner, know how to work well with others, and model exemplary practice. He or she must have the skills to provide direct support daily to the intern and be given the time, the materials, and the support necessary to carry out those tasks. The mentor completes the necessary evaluative material and monitors the intern's progress. He or she must attest to the intern's successful completion of the program.

The school principal must recognize the important purpose that the internship serves, support the efforts of the mentor, and nourish the activities of the intern. The principal also completes routine evaluations of the intern.

The staff development coordinator has overall responsibility for the program and serves as a source of information on the required course work and the alternative certification route.

The curriculum specialist teaches the curriculum and methods courses required, verifies the successful implementation of the curriculum and methods component (in conjunction with the mentor), and provides expertise and resources that the mentor teacher may lack.

For more information, contact the Division of Teacher Education, State Department of Education, Twin Towers East, Atlanta, GA 30334, 404/656-2431.

Indiana
Project CREDIT
Indiana State University in collaboration with 10 school districts

Indiana State University's Project CREDIT (Certification Renewal Experiences Designed to Improve Teaching) is a joint program developed by the university's Department of Secondary Education and 10 school districts in west-central Indiana. Its major objectives are to improve the skills and reduce the problems of beginning teachers, reduce burnout and dropout, and reward superior teachers. The program is guided by a steering committee of three teachers, two school administrators, and two university professors, who developed the procedures for program design and now provide direction and guidelines for personnel.

First-year teachers are assigned a mentor, who is an outstanding teacher according to criteria established by the steering committee. The mentor offers support by providing orientation, helping with problem solving, and conducting formative evaluations. University supervisors assist through monthly site visits, classroom observations, and consultation with mentors, beginning teachers (called interns), and principals. A group of university consultants assists in human relations, classroom management and discipline, testing and evaluating of students, methods and techniques of instruction, and use of the computer in instruction. Peer support is provided through a human relations orientation program, a monthly dinner seminar, and a newsletter.

For more information, contact Marvin A. Henry, chair, Department of Secondary Education, Indiana State University, Terre Haute, IN 47809.

New Hampshire
One-Year Internship in Teaching
University of New Hampshire

The University of New Hampshire (UNH) internship program is part of a five-year teacher education program that includes an undergraduate major other than education, an early field experience designed to assist students in making a realistic career choice, a core of professional course options, graduate work leading to a master's degree, and a full-year internship in the student's fifth year. The one-year internship serves to bridge the gap between theory and practice and is credited by most school districts as a full year of teaching. All interns must complete the baccalaureate degree and be accepted into the UNH teacher certification or master's degree program before the internship.

Secondary school candidates typically have majored in the subject area they intend to teach. Elementary school candidates vary in their majors, but often have a heavy emphasis in the social sciences.

The placement of interns begins in early spring before the internship year. Interns share responsibility for choosing a cooperating teacher. The match of intern and cooperating teacher is considered very important and is based on common professional interests and potential for personal compatibility.

A university supervisor is assigned to work with six or more interns and their cooperating teachers. The supervisor visits the interns on site at least six times each semester, initiates a minimum of four three-way evaluative conferences, meets weekly with interns in an extended seminar, and meets biweekly with other supervisors as a group to share concerns and formulate policy.

For more information, contact Judith A. Krull or Michael D. Andrew, Department of Education, Morrill Hall, University of New Hampshire, Durham, NH 03824, 603/862-3557 or 862-2310.

New Mexico
Teacher Induction Program
Albuquerque Public Schools and the University of New Mexico

The Albuquerque–University of New Mexico Teacher Induction Program is conceived as a model of school system–university collaboration to offer assistance to all beginning teachers in Albuquerque's 76 elementary and 34 secondary schools. The university provides 46 graduate interns to serve as first-year teachers. The school system releases 24 veterans to support both the graduate interns and the system's beginning teachers. The program is directed by a university faculty member whose salary is paid jointly by the university and the school district. The objective is to support elementary and secondary school teachers new to the profession in the transition from college student to practitioner. The program includes supporting personal adjustment and instructional effectiveness, and fostering the retention of beginning teachers.

The 24 veterans, known as clinical support teachers, are selected jointly by the school system and the university. Their primary responsibility is to assist beginners. They have no responsibility for evaluation connected with job continuance, tenure, or certification. Beginners can feel free to share strengths and weaknesses in a nonjudgmental climate. Support teachers offer personal support and in-class consultation, counsel beginners on methods and materials, and demonstrate teaching techniques. They also furnish information and consultation on school policies, procedures, curriculum, testing, and other school matters.

In their clinical role, support teachers have an opportunity to be students of the teaching process and of the school system. They receive their regular teacher's salary and fringe benefits plus waivers on tuition for university courses. Typically they return to a regular teaching assignment after one year.

Beginning teachers have the option of attending workshops planned around the needs they identify. University credit for such inservice training is available.

For more information, contact Sandra J. Odell, director, Elementary Graduate Intern and Teacher Induction Program, College of Education, University of New Mexico, Albuquerque, NM 87131, 505/277-4114.

North Carolina

Initial Certification Program

North Carolina Department of Public Instruction

Assistance to the beginning teacher is a part of the North Carolina Initial Certification Program, which in turn is a piece of the State's Quality Assurance Program. The overall goal is to improve teaching effectiveness by extending the preparation of teachers to six years (four years preservice and two years probationary) and by changing the certification procedure. The program, which became effective in the 1984–85 school year, calls for granting new teachers an initial certificate upon graduation from an approved teacher education program and issuing them a continuing certificate after demonstration of competence in performance as measured by the state's Teacher Performance Appraisal System/Initial Certification (TPAS/IC).

The Initial Certification Program is designed to support a beginner's professional growth during the first two years of employment. Support involves assignment of a mentor or a support team (to provide guidance and counsel and to promote assimilation into the profession), development of a professional development plan (PDP) by the beginner and the mentor or the support team on the basis of observations using the TPAS/IC, and documentation in the form of a portfolio. The latter includes the PDP; a record of the strengths and the areas of development determined from observation; a summative data report with ratings, support team summary, and teacher comments at the end of each year; and evidence of completion of the strategies in the PDP.

If a mentor is deemed to be the appropriate support person, the principal or his or her designee shares the responsibility for providing assistance. If a support team is formed to assist, it must include (but not be limited to) a career-status teacher, the principal or a designee, and a generalist or a specialist in curriculum and instruction (who may be a higher education or central office person).

The responsibility of mentors or support teams includes assessing the performance of initially certified personnel and facilitating the development and the refinement of essential practices and skills. In that work they conduct conferences, make observations and confer about performance as measured on the TPAS/IC, make copies of formative and summative assessments available to assist in preparing the PDP, give general feedback and assistance on growth and development, provide a link to appropriate technical assistance, and ensure that appropriate data are included in the beginners' portfolios.

Program guidelines require that mentors and support team members be carefully selected according to criteria and procedures developed locally in collaboration with higher education institutions, that selection be made jointly by the superintendent of schools (or his or her designee) and the school principal, and that if possible, career teachers be from the same school, level, and subject area as the beginners whom they guide. Also, career teachers must have the knowledge and be able to demonstrate the competencies expected of beginners, as well as demonstrating the skills required of effective mentors or support team members. Local education agencies are responsible for the appropriate training of mentors and support team members. Actual training is to be designed and delivered as a collaborative effort with the North Carolina Department of Public Instruction and higher education institutions.

The recommended components of training for mentors and support team members are orientation and clarification of roles, observation skills using the TPAS/IC, conferencing skills, theories of adult development, effective teaching practices, and development of a professional development plan.

Upon successful completion of all certification requirements and recommendation from an employer with an approved plan, the employee is eligible for continuing certification and further career growth in the profession. Certification decisions are legally and clearly separate from employment decisions. Each is seen as having a different purpose.

The Nash and Wake County programs, described next, meet the state requirements and illustrate the approach taken by two North Carolina counties that have chosen year-long training for mentors. Many North Carolina school districts have a much shorter period of training.

For more information, contact Jean Blackmun, Division of Program Approval, State Department of Education, Raleigh, NC 27611, 919/733-4736.

The Novice Teacher and the Mentor
Nash County

To carry out the state mandate for induction of beginning teachers, Nash County has established a systematic and intensive program to train mentor teachers, who assist and assess beginning teachers. Teachers must apply to be mentors. Once accepted, they must be trained in the state's Effective Teacher Training and Performance Appraisal programs. The role of the mentor is to assess the demonstrated performance of the novice teacher and to facilitate the development and the refinement of essential practices and skills. To prepare for the role, prospective mentors must develop skills in observation and analysis of teaching, conferencing, assisting in the formation of a professional development plan for the novice, and membership on a support team. The state mandate does not require the mentor to have direct responsibility for employment decisions relating to the beginning teacher. But as a support team member, the mentor is one of the assessors who determine whether or not certification will be granted.

In the state plan the mentor is included in formative evaluations and conferences, but usually does not participate in summative evaluations. Nash County does include mentors in the summative appraisal because evidence suggests that they serve as advocates of beginning teachers and have maintained cooperative relationships with beginners.

Mentors in Nash County were initially prepared in a semester-long course at North Carolina State University (NCSU). NCSU has since provided training for the trainers of mentors, so that Nash County now has qualified teachers who prepare their peers for the mentor role. The course is followed by a year-long practicum during which mentors practice their skills with colleagues. They meet no less than seven times over the year to share ideas and refine techniques. Other follow-up activities include networking meetings at NCSU and in the school district to stay updated on training materials.

The Nash County program prepares prospective mentors to build a helping relationship with beginners. It includes the study of adult development, coaching techniques, and other mentoring strategies. Preparing mentors to both support and challenge the beginning teacher to grow and to improve is unique to the county.

For more information, contact Larry Lugar, director, Middle Grades and Computer Education, Nash County School System, 930 Eastern Avenue, Nashville, NC 27856, 919/459-7021.

Mentor/Novice Program
Wake County

The Wake County program is designed to help new teachers find success and satisfaction. Mentors assist beginners in applying their training to the real world of students and classrooms. They help with such matters as learning to know students, becoming oriented to the faculty and the curriculum, arranging content to fit learning styles and student interests, demonstrating effective teaching practices, and learning the routines and the policies of the district.

To accomplish this, Wake County provides a two-year induction period for all new teachers. The purpose is to accelerate teacher development. The program, which dovetails with North Carolina's two-year probationary period, has four features: assistance from a highly trained mentor teacher, fall and spring seminars in the first year (through a New Teacher Institute), beginning teacher support groups, and time to observe the best teachers in the system. The attempt is to make staff development a continuous effort, linking preservice training, induction, and career-long growth.

The key feature is the mentor. Mentors are experienced, highly competent teachers who have been given a year of specialized training to work with beginners. Teachers selected for this role must be recommended by their peers and their principal, have received outstanding ratings for the previous three years, have at least five years of teaching experience, be committed to educational innovation, and believe in the helping role.

One mentor is assigned to each beginner. Mentors' responsibilities are usually add-ons to a regular teaching load. They teach in the same building as the beginners with whom they work. When possible, mentors and beginners with similar subject-matter expertise are paired. Both the mentor and the novice are assigned the equivalent of five days for the two to plan together, for the mentor to observe the novice, for the novice to observe experienced teachers, and for the novice to participate in the New Teacher Institute. In secondary schools the planning period is often also used for these purposes.

The Wake County program has been in operation for five years and is becoming institutionalized. It is affiliated with North Carolina State University (NCSU). NCSU faculty have provided training for mentors and trainers of mentors, so that Wake County now has over 500 qualified mentor teachers who can support and assist student teachers, beginning teachers, and colleagues.

The school-university relationship has developed to the point that a coordinator position has been created for the beginning teacher program as a joint appointment. A former teacher, mentor, and mentor trainer in Wake County currently holds the position.

Wake County and NCSU personnel believe that both helping and evaluating the beginner are important, but have separated the two. To make it easier for mentors to gain the confidence and the trust of beginning teachers, the district has designated the building-level administrator as the evaluator of performance. Mentors are engaged only in formative work with beginners.

For more information, contact Alan Reiman, Wake County Public Schools, Staff Development Office, 3600 Wake Forest Road, Raleigh, NC 27511, 919/790-2421.

Tennessee

MAT Internship Program

Memphis State University

The Memphis State program is a 15-month postbaccalaureate teacher education program that combines elements of preparation and induction. Now in its fourth year, it is characterized by three unique features: moving participants through the program in cohorts; accommodating late entrants to teaching (liberal arts graduates who choose a career in education after earning a bachelor's degree); and focusing on prospective secondary school teachers. Candidates are admitted once a year. They are supported by practitioner mentors from the schools and pedagogical mentors from the college.

The internship occurs in three phases, over the course of which interns assume increasing responsibility as teachers. In the first phase the interns, who are called teacher assistants, are involved in a structured field experience. They complete two assignments in junior and senior high schools that differ in demographic and socioeconomic characteristics. Each assignment is approximately three weeks long, four hours per day. The teacher assistants study student behavior; observe exemplary teaching; review curriculum materials; and plan, teach, and evaluate a sequence of three or four lessons. These experiences serve as a laboratory for college classes that the interns are completing in classroom management, special methods, and social foundations.

In the second phase the interns, now called teacher associates, move to a different school and are progressively immersed in the role of classroom teacher. Gradually they assume partial teaching loads (three classes) as quasi-independent professionals. This occurs during the last half of the fall semester. Priority is given to the interns' instructional responsibilities, and close attention is paid to their growth in classroom management, assessment of student progress, rapport with colleagues, and command of subject matter.

The teacher experience, the third phase, comes during the spring semester. Interns become a part of a faculty in a full-day semester-long assignment, normally in the same school as in the second phase and with the same practitioner mentor. The typical responsibility is two classes as the teacher-of-record, two periods working in the classroom with their practitioner mentor (ideally a team-teaching arrangement), and two preparation periods. For the two periods as teacher-of-record, interns assume the full range of teaching responsibilities and are encouraged to experiment with new strategies. Two preparation periods are provided because, in addition to teaching, interns enrolled in a graduate program are required to complete a thesis, which entails data collection.

Pedagogical mentors, from the college, each work with several interns and serve as members of thesis committees. They observe the interns in the three phases of the program, assist with a professional development seminar, and consult with school personnel on interns' progress. They serve as critic, counselor, advisor, teacher, role model, resource person, and advocate. They see their interns teach approximately 12 times over the course of the program and meet with them formally or informally nearly every week.

The practitioner mentors each work with one intern during phases two and three. They critique their intern's school-based work, introduce the intern to others, advise him or her regarding school politics, provide exposure, serve as an advocate and a defender in the school environment, and consult with the pedagogical mentor. Practitioner mentors have a partially reduced teaching load because one or two of their classes are those for which the intern becomes the teacher-of-record. Also, mentors have access to backup support from specialists at the university and in the local school system.

The technical, psychological, and professional support that interns derive from the members of their cohort is immeasurable. The experience builds a network that interns carry into professional practice.

For more information, contact Terry L. James, College of Education, Memphis State University, Memphis, TN 38152, 901/454-2351.

Virginia

Teachers Need Teachers
Chesterfield County Schools, Virginia Polytechnic Institute and
State University, and the Virginia Department of Education

The Teachers Need Teachers (TNT) program is a collaborative
effort of the Virginia Department of Education, the Chesterfield
County Schools, and the College of Education, Virginia Polytechnic Institute and State University. TNT follows a successful
two-year pilot program conducted by the school district and the
university. The program's premises are that special support systems provided by mentors can aid beginners as they learn about
teaching on the job during their first year, and that if beginners
adapt acceptably, they are likely to become skillful teachers and
choose to stay in the profession.

TNT emphasizes selection and preparation of mentors. The
focus of preparation is on (a) developing a concept of mentoring,
(b) improving communication skills (including discussing the act
of teaching and giving nonjudgmental feedback based on observation), (c) analyzing the complexity of teaching through case
study discussions and reflection, (d) raising consciousness of
professional language used in talking about teaching, and (e)
reviewing problems of beginning teachers and learning ways to
aid in effective problem solving. The function of the mentor is to
help the beginner learn about teaching, reduce the work load, feel
good about teaching, and become integrated into the school
community.

Each mentor is assigned one beginner. The program for beginners includes day-to-day monitoring, release days, area meetings,
and interviews through which mentors help beginners in various
ways. Mentoring occurs formally and informally. Mentors listen,
share materials, offer helpful hints, give time, act as models, serve
as brokers, respond to questions, provide feedback, promote reflection, plan cooperatively, and assist in problem solving.

Principals are recognized as having important roles in TNT, the
most important one being helping select an appropriate mentor

for the beginner. They also facilitate collaboration between beginners and mentors, understanding that there is no single, ideal mentoring relationship.

For more information, contact Margaret Hable, coordinator, Chesterfield County Public Schools, Chesterfield, VA 23832, 804/748-1719, or Terry Wildman, College of Education, Virginia Polytechnic Institute and State University, Blacksburg, VA 24061, 703/231-5598.

West Virginia
Teacher Induction Program
Ohio County Schools

The goal of the Ohio County program is to assist teachers in developing confidence in themselves and pride in and commitment to their school system and profession. Goals are achieved by enhancing the instructional skills of new teachers, developing a strong collegial network, and ensuring that new teachers are fully informed about school district issues and policies. The program began in 1980; in 1987–88, 55 teachers participated.

All teachers new to the school system are required to participate in a three-year developmental program of support and assistance. In the first year they are assigned mentors from among content-area supervisors in the central office. For the first nine weeks, mentors follow a series of activities set forth in the district's mentor handbook, including school visits (to total about 20 over the first year), phone calls, and notes. After this initial period the level of mentor involvement diminishes. New teachers also participate in five two-and-a-half-hour seminars each school year. Separate seminars may be offered to true novices and experienced teachers new to the system. Each new teacher receives an induction notebook (which contains information on school policy, personnel matters, and curriculum) and a quarterly newsletter.

Second- and third-year teachers have opportunities to observe peers. Their observation focuses on teaching behaviors and classroom characteristics that are illustrative of effective teaching. They record positive examples of these behaviors and characteristics, and the collected data serve as material for induction seminars. In the third year either a supervisor, a principal, or a department chair observes the new teacher engaging in a selected teaching behavior or strategy based on effective schools research. All new teachers keep their own professional portfolios according to school district guidelines. The portfolios include communications to and from parents; evidence of students' academic progress or special activities; records of continuing education, committee service, professional memberships, and citations and awards; and newspaper clippings.

For more information, contact Mary Marockie, Regional Education Service Agency VI, or Lawrence M. Miller, Ohio County Schools, Wheeling, WV 26003, 304/243-0440.

Wisconsin
Program for Mentoring Teachers
Wisconsin Department of Public Instruction

The recommendation for an Entry-Year Assistance Program in Wisconsin came from the Task Force on Teaching and Teacher Education appointed by the state superintendent of public instruction. All first-year teachers, the Task Force said, should participate in a one-year induction program occurring under the auspices of the Department of Public Instruction (DPI) and involving personnel from the local school district and an institution of higher education. Five induction models, funded through the DPI's Teaching Incentive Pilot Program, have been pilot-tested:

1. University-centered model. This model requires the first-year teacher and his or her mentor to take a three-credit course, prepare a weekly written report, and participate in monthly seminars. Also, the first-year teacher must be closely supervised by a university faculty member. Developed exclusively by the university, the program is highly structured.

2. Residency model. Under the residency model the first-year teacher assumes a lighter load and receives two-thirds salary, carries 12 graduate credits, and is assigned a men-

tor teacher. The program includes a monthly seminar held in the school district. Also developed and directed by the university, the model gives the district great leeway in planning the seminars and administering the program.

3. District-centered model. This model was developed exclusively by a local district advisory council consisting of teachers, administrators, school board representatives, and community members. It features mentors, monthly seminars, informal social gatherings, and end-of-year evaluations by building administrators. No college credit is given; the university is minimally involved.

4. University-district cooperative plan. Developed by a university and a school district, but administered by the district, this plan involves university faculty serving as consultants to mentors and first-year teachers. No college credit is involved.

5. Consortium model. This model is based on a university campus, but administered by a consortium of school districts. Four liaison master teachers are granted leave from their districts to work in the Regional Staff Development Center on the university campus. One liaison mentor teacher is assigned primary responsibility for assisting teachers. Each beginning teacher is paired with a mentor in his or her building and a cooperating building supervisor. The university plays a supportive role.

The pilots substantiated the need for an assistance program and resulted in some common guidelines, among them the following:

- A mentor should provide assistance to the beginning teacher.
- A faculty member from a preparing institution should be assigned to work with the beginning teacher.
- There should be a training workshop for the induction team that addresses the following topics: problems of first-year teachers, supervision and staff development, facilitating the learning of adults, and performance assessment.
- A beginning teacher program may include the following: beginning-year orientation, monthly seminars based on a

needs assessment, development of a personal development plan by the first-year teacher (under the guidance of the induction team), and a performance assessment by the building administrator and a university consultant. (Performance assessment instruments are being piloted by the Training Incentives Pilot Program.)

In January 1989 the DPI issued a publication entitled *Report of the State Superintendent's Advisory Committee on Beginning Teacher Assistance Programs,* which is available from the address below.

For more information, contact Kathryn Lind, director, Teacher Induction Program, Department of Public Instruction, P.O. Box 7841, Madison, WI 53707-7841.